PUBS
BARS & CLUBS
handbook

Messer Drinks Dispense is at the forefront of helping licensees with advice on recent government legislation affecting the trade. Confined Spaces Regulations came into force in January 1998, and requires all employers to make an assessment of specific risks which exist when entering a confined space, primarily your cellar. By working with the HSE and various trade bodies Messer ensure that support and advice is available for all, to assist with adherence to the regulations. Simple risk assessment sheets are available from Messer Drinks Dispense to initially help you identify the level of risk. These forms are used to calculate a value, which quantifies the volume of gas from the largest cylinder connected in the cellar, as a percentage of the total volume of free air space within the cellar. This percentage value gives an indication of the level of risk as set by the HSE which are detailed as – Low, Medium or High risk. From the findings it may be deemed that a full risk assessment is required by a trained competent person. They will conduct the full risk assessment and advise on any remedial action that needs to be implented. This will include guidance on training and emergency procedures. In certain cases recommendations may include the installation of an expensive forced air extraction system or the simple installation of a CO_2 monitor. The CO_2 monitor has both visual and audible warning alarms external to the cellar. Alarms are installed at all entrances at risk ensuring that if a gas leak has occurred no one enters the cellar and the emergency procedures can be implemented.

Whilst this all appears to be very complicated it is mainly common sense with the first stage of assessment being just a phone call away. Messer Drinks Dispense has all the information available to assist you with compliance. Call us on **0800 917 1313** today and we will recommend the best way forward to provide a safe working environment for everyone on your premises.

Messer Drinks Dispense are a company with a proud tradition of being able to offer the licensed trade the tools it needs to dispense beers, lagers, ciders and postmix in their optimum state using the method best suited for your establishment. Using either CO_2, pre-mixed cylinders or our market leading On Site Generation system, Messer cater for National Retailers, Regional Brewers and thousands of individual site operators. As the largest supplier of CO_2 in the UK, we work closely with the HSE and various trade bodies to ensure that you receive upto date advice concerning government legislation relating to dispense gases. Our extensive product and service range provides all the benefits that come with using one of the leading brands of drinks dispense gases.

1. Full range of pre-mixed cylinders and CO_2 used by all the National Brewers backed by the knowledge that you are purchasing a product that has been subject to the most stringent quality checks and controls unparalleled in the industry

2. Advice on Confined Spaces Regulations, how to implement procedures and equipment to ensure that you meet with the legislation

3. National cylinder distribution network providing reliable and efficient local service

4. Market leading On Site Nitrogen Generation systems, with thousands installed nationally in both managed, freetrade and tenanted sites backed by 365 day per year technical support

5. Dedicated to developing products and services for the future benefit of the industry

6. Contract filling and gas analysis service for companies filling their own cylinders

Please contact Messer Drinks Dispense on **0800 637737** to find out how Messer can provide the solutions you need to meet your drinks dispense requirements.

Behind **every good pint** is a **Messer** drinks dispense gas cylinder

With Messer drinks dispense gases you're guaranteed a full measure of customer commitment, plus all the benefits that come with using one of the leading brands of drinks dispense gases. Call us today and find out how our service is pints ahead of the competition.

By dealing with Messer UK:

⊕ You can feel safe in the knowledge that all gases, cylinders and equipment comply with health and safety legislation and regulatory requirements

⊕ You are placing your requirements in the hands of the largest supplier of CO_2 in the UK

⊕ You are dealing with market leaders in on-site nitrogen drinks dispense systems

⊕ You have access to an extensive product range to satisfy all drinks dispense requirements

FOR FURTHER INFORMATION CONTACT MESSER UK ON **FREEPHONE 0800 917 131**

Messer UK Marketing Department, Station Road, Coleshill, Birmingham, B46 1JY
Tel 0800 917 1313 Fax (01675) 467022 www.messer.co.uk gen.enq@messer.co.uk

MESSER ⊕

PUBS
6th edition
BARS & CLUBS
handbook

Formerly the *Publican's Handbook*

*advice & ideas for running a
successful licensed business*

consultant editor: danny blyth

Dewberry Boyes

JohnsonDiversey
Clean is just the beginning

KOGAN
PAGE

First published as *The Publican's Handbook* in 1997
This sixth edition published in 2003

Kogan Page Limited
120 Pentonville Road
London N1 9JN
www.kogan-page.co.uk

© Kogan Page and Contributors 2003

British Library Cataloguing in Publication Data

ISBN 0 7494 4053 8

Typeset by JS Typesetting Ltd, Wellingborough, Northants.
Printed and bound in Great Britain by Cambrian Printers, Wales.

REFRIGERATION

Cooling, freezing, ice- making, air conditioning, climate control or just plain chilling out – by any other name its still **REFRIGERATION.**

So what's the big deal, we have all got at least one. Well, that *is* the deal, think about it. No refrigeration means no cold beer, no chilled wines, warm salads and food ready to walk instead of eat.

We are, in today's world, totally dependent on refrigeration whether we like it or not. No, its not just that box with glass doors behind the bar (you know, the one where you forget to close the doors or even leave them open to cool your feet).

Refrigeration is everywhere. It keeps the baby milk at the start of life and "keeps you fresh" at the end of your life. Blood banks, ice cream, insulin, cold beer, carbon fibre for aircraft, airline meals, shipments for New Zealand lamb (that was the *first* refrigerated shipment!), chilled water coolers, banana ripening rooms and the 'fridge/freezer' in your kitchen. The list is endless.

So why is the humble, and much maligned fridge the last equipment to be thought of?

So many architects and specifiers leave it till last and then squeeze in a small one. So many buyers concentrate on the pretty stuff in front of house. A fridge? Oh yeah, we can get *one* later (and then forget that the fresh and cooked meats should not be kept together).

Your refrigeration equipment is probably the only item on your premises that you expect to work 24 hours a day, 7 days a week, 52 weeks a year. But do you look after it? Do you clean it enough? Do you maintain it properly? (Yes, I know good service costs, but you service your car don't you?)

On the subject of cars, someone better at maths than me once calculated how many miles a fridge compressor does compared to a car engine, all based on RPM (revolutions per minute!) Assuming the actual running time (of a well-maintained compressor is about 16/18 hours out of 24 it was calculated that the compressor travels the equivalent of over 250,000 miles *every* year. Now, when was your fridge last serviced and how often between services on your car. Also just like a car, poor maintenance means higher running costs and a shorter life.

So how can you get the most from your refrigeration equipment? Let's go right back to the start.

THE DECISION
Believe me, all fridges are not created equal. There are LADA's, FORD's and MERCEDES with everything in between.

Don't skimp; buy the best you can afford for the job you want it to do. Check what's around, you might not need to be like 'Label Lil'. Check, is that kitchen fridge really stainless steel or does it just look like stainless steel?

If you are keeping different food products you may need 2 cabinets, or at least a combi.

OK, you've got room in the kitchen but will it come through the door, up or down the stiars, can it turn round that tight corner? This is important. You have got food regulations but your supplier also has health and safety regulations that cover equipment handling. If you're not sure *please* discuss it with your supplier *before* placing the order. This is a major purchase and you want it right.

THE DELIVERY

OK, so it's arriving today, have you cleared the site and access? Is the 13-amp socket in the right place? Regulations forbid extending cables and the switch should be accessible in case you need to switch it off (for cleaning!) Just as you don't want to wait for a truck that's held up on a previous delivery, remember the driver will have a redundant 'fridge to dispose of' it must be done legally and yes it does cost money. Please to it correctly and think of the environment.

THE INSTALLATION

It's in place, levelled and ready to go. No, you didn't put it next to the fryer or fan heater did you? Please clean it before you use and allow the correct temperature to be obtained *before* loading. Read the information supplied, fit the shelves to suit your products and load it up. DON'T overfill and block internal airways because half your product won't be cold enough. A storage fridge or a back bar cooler is not a blast chiller, it takes time to reduce product temperature. How long? We are always asked.

Well, that depends on many factors, how warm is the incoming product, will you leave the doors closed etc etc.

THE USE (NOT MISUSE)

Never obstruct internal and external airways. That grill on the front or the open top on kitchen equipment is for a good reason. Dependent on location, always check the condenser monthly and clean as required. If a cleanable filter is used, clean and replace properly. Don't load with warm food, and always close the door properly. Your fridge may have a visual thermometer, remember, this is the air temperature not the product temperature. The air temperature may rise if the door is in heavy use but the product temperature does not change as quickly. If you think you have a problem close the doors and leave for 20 minutes and see if normal temperature resumes.

THE CLEANING

Good, you purchased a fridge or freezer with automatic defrost *but* – don't forget auto defrost is not auto cleaning. At least every 3 months switch off the cabinet and completely empty it. Remove any shelves, supports, grills etc and clean those also. Ensure all items and the interior are dry before switching the fridge back on.

A PROBLEM

If you think you have a problem don't panic. Do not phone your service company until you check the most basic items. Is it plugged in and switched on, is the fuse OK, is it just on a defrost cycle. It is very common for these kind of "faults" to be found by an engineer and guarantees and service contracts don't cover it, it can get expensive for you!

THE RESULT

Buy the right equipment, treat it well and in the vast majority of cases your purchase will serve you well for many years and save you money as well.

Mick Welch, *40 years in refrigeration and still learning*

Contents

Develop your expertise in wines and spirits

at Westminster Kingsway College

Throughout the year, our prestigious School of Hospitality offers a range of programmes that lead to qualifications designed for those employed in the licensed trade, or those who wish to further their personal interest and knowledge of wines, spirits and other alcoholic beverages. All the courses take place in the "Lyndsey Wine Centre" at our Vincent Square site near Victoria.

BIIAB National Licensee Certificate (Off Licence)

This one-and-a-half day course runs regularly every month and covers the basic law and social responsibilities of licensees. Candidates should be working or aspiring to work in the the licensed sector.
Fee for all students £169

BIIAB National Licensee Certificate (On-Licence and Part IV)

This version of the Certificate is also a one-and-a-half day course and runs every week during term time. Candidates should be already working or aspiring to work in the the licensed sector.
Fee for all students £169

Wine & Spirit Education Trust Intermediate Certificate

This termly ten-week course covers the theory of wine production, tasting technique and service. It runs on Tuesday evenings from 6-8pm.
Fee for all students £200
including registration, exam fee and tastings.

Wine & Spirit Education Trust Advanced Certificate

This advanced 16-week course in the art of wine appreciation is available for people who want to progress from the Intermediate Certificate. It is also a good background for those wishing to study for the diploma. It runs on Wednesday evenings from 6-8pm.
Fee for all students £250
including registration, exam fee and tastings.

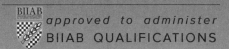

BIIAB *approved to administer* BIIAB QUALIFICATIONS

For details and how to enrol please contact
Karishma Mistri on **020 7802 8399**
Or you can contact Course Information on

020 7556 8001

Email **courseinfo@westking.ac.uk**
Web **www.westking.ac.uk**

Westminster Kingsway College

educating for life

The Contributors

Martin Armitt is Trade Marketing Manager for Douwe Egbert's Coffee Systems, responsible for marketing across a range of sectors that include pubs, hotels, restaurants, staff catering and leisure. After graduating in 1994, he went to work in a trade marketing capacity for Rothmans UK for six years, prior to taking his present position. He is married with one child and lives in Buckinghamshire.

Danny Blyth is now in his 20th year as a journalist and consultant specialising in licensed retailing and catering. He has regular columns in the *Pub Business* magazine, *Restaurant Business* and *Cost Sector Catering* and is a frequent contributor to other trade and business titles as well as consumer publications like *Whisky Magazine* and *Scotland Magazine*. In addition, he contributes to the in-house publications of pub groups and brands like Budweiser. He has also acted as a consultant to the industry on everything from brand launches to incentive schemes and even on raising investment capital. He is married, lives in Newbury and fancies himself as a chef. Email: danny.blyth@virgin.net

Ted Bruning has been a journalist working in the licensed trade and beer consumer press for over 15 years, and is also the author of a number of books on pubs and beer including *Historic Pubs of London* and *Historic Inns of England*. He is currently Editor of the Campaign for Real Ale's national membership newspaper, *What's Brewing*. Ted is 45 and lives in Cambridgeshire with his wife and two children.

Richard Castleton is the Head of Human Resources for the Retail Division of Hall & Woodhouse Badger Brewery in Blandford in Dorset. During the short time Richard has been with the company he has implemented new training and recruitment initiatives to move the business into the 21st century.

Richard's previous experiences range from six years as an Officer in the Army Catering Corps to nearly four years with Allied Domecq's pub estate in the late 1990s. Claims to fame in human resources include a positive action report for West Yorkshire Police and recently bringing chefs from abroad to fill a gap in the market.

Isabella Gambuzzi is the Managing Director of the Mediterranean ingredients supplier iB Food Plc. Her passion for food stems from a childhood spent in her parent's Italian restaurants in south London. It was here, and during long summers in Italy, that her interest in all things food developed, and to make a career in the catering industry was therefore a natural progression.

In 1987, Isabella and her late husband Carlo identified a niche opportunity to supply authentic Mediterranean chef ingredients to the UK food service trade and so formed iB Food. The objective was to encourage increased popularity of Italian cuisine. This was achieved by bringing in speciality items, all of which are sourced direct from artisan producers in Italy, and are made to traditional regional recipes using home-made or local produce.

Matthew Hudson has worked in the UK wine industry since 1982 for a number of wholesalers, most recently (since 1993) for Oddbins Corporate Business, the trade supply arm of Oddbins. He holds the Wine & Spirit Education Trust Diploma, has a keen interest in alcoholic beverages of all shapes and sizes and operates a small brewery in his back garden.

When **Les Leonard** ran a Kentish pub back in the early 1970s, the menu consisted of a few curled up sandwiches – cheese, ham and liver sausage – and a couple of main courses – either steak and kidney pie or fish and chips, both with chips. And the wine list was the best that Grants of St James could offer – Nicholas white, red and rosé. Pub culinary and drinks delights have certainly progressed in the last three decades!

After being brought up on a farm adjoining Sir Winston Churchill's Chartwell country estate, Les joined the local Sevenoaks weekly, which was later taken over by Associated Newspapers. A colleague on the regional rag joined the *Morning Advertiser*, then a daily paper dating back to 1784 and serving the pub and brewing industry. When the friend returned to Les's local after a day out extolling the virtues of the latest day interviewing a busty landlady or being at a brewery launch and 'sampling' vast quantities of cask ale, the ex-licensee was keen to serve the 'Barmaid's Bible'. The opportunity arose in 1979, and for the next 20 years Les had what he described as the 'perfect post' covering pub trade stories in London and the south east, from the Kent coast to the New Forest. Three years ago he joined Dewberry Boyes, publishers of *Restaurant Business*, and also writes for the sister magazine *Pub Business*.

John McNamara was appointed as Chief Executive of the British Institute of Innkeeping (BII) on January 2, 2002. He was previously Director of the Hospitality

Training Foundation (HtF). John has a wide commercial background gained in the financial services industry and in training and development, and is also Chairman of the UK Federation of Awarding Bodies, which represents 44 members to the regulators, funding authorities and other key influence groups. John's remit as Chief Executive is to achieve a growing membership base, to offer unbeatable membership benefits and to ensure nationwide acceptance of its superb and evolving range of professional qualifications.

Jackie Mitchell is a seasoned food and travel writer. She trained as a journalist in the UK with IPC Magazines and Reed Business Information and worked on publications such as *Caterer & Hotelkeeper*, *Travel Weekly* and *Homes and Gardens* magazine. She then moved to Hong Kong, where she was Editor of *Travelnews Asia* and PR Manager of Holiday Inn Asia/Pacific, which gave her a real insight into the hospitality industry. She has also worked on magazines and newspapers in Australia and New York, USA. Her travel books include *Long Stays in Australia*.

Since her return to the UK, Jackie has written about the hospitality and catering industry for over 10 years. During that time, she has edited several publications including *European Hotelier* and *Independent Hotelier*, which won a 'Helping Hands Award' from the Federation of Small Businesses.

Jackie writes regularly for trade publications on the latest trends in food and drink and reports widely on food exhibitions. She writes profiles on catering operations and restaurants and interviews key players in the industry.

Jackie lives with her husband in Surrey and has two stepdaughters, who are vegetarian. Email: words@jackiem.com

Dominic Roskrow is the Editor of *Whisky Magazine* and *Scotland Magazine*, and has been writing about the drinks trade for 12 years. He edited *Pub Food* and *Pub Business* and was Features Editor on *The Publican* newspaper. He has also written for a range of specialist publications and Internet companies, and currently contributes to *Acclaim*, the in-house magazine of the Laurel Pub Company. He is married and has two young boys, but is still an unrefined heavy rock and alternative country music fan, and supports Leicester City and the All Blacks loudly and a lot – especially when he's drinking whisky.

Bob Russell is the proprietor of J.C. Signs & Scenes, which is one of the very few sign companies in Britain that specialises in traditional signs, and the only one accepted by The Craft Council. Bob's studio is on licensed premises as his wife (BII member) Sandie is the licensee of the Johns Cross Inn, a freehouse on the A21 in East Sussex. Bob's speciality is gold and platinum leaf, heraldic and pictorial commissions which have ranged from extensive work in the licensed trade, special orders from abroad, heraldic work for The Commonwealth War Grave Commission, to decorative gilding at the Apollo Theatre for Andrew Lloyd Webber. Contact him at www.jc-signsandscenes.co.uk

Ker...ching!

The wonderful sound of plastic

These days, all kinds of people prefer to pay with all kinds of plastic – because then they won't be limited to the amount of cash they're carrying. So catering for every card is more likely to keep those tills ringing – and give your profits a boost. That's where we come in.

Barclaycard Merchant Services can provide a card processing system that's suited to your business. We offer a range of terminals, all of which are fast, compact, easy to use and equipped with the latest Chip and PIN technology to guard against fraud.

To find out more, please contact us. We'll talk through your options with you, and help ensure we find the right solution for your business – and your customers.

Kerching.

Call **0800 328 3299***
quoting reference PCHB04

Lines open 8.30am – 6pm, Monday – Friday
*Calls may be monitored or recorded for training purposes.

Since graduating from Brunel University with a degree in International Business Studies, **Karen Salters** started the Marketing Department at Beverage Brands. Today there are 25 people within the team and Karen is the Marketing Manager for Beverage Brands UK Ltd, overseeing the marketing and brand management of the portfolio of brands WKD, WKD 40, Woody's Vodka Refresher, Joe's Club Cocktails and Caledonian Clear.

Simon Speers is Managing Director at Bottle Green Drinks Co., the innovative adult leisure drink producer based in Gloucestershire. Formerly Head of Britvic International, Simon has a wealth of soft drinks expertise and a sound understanding of the on-trade

Following senior sales and marketing positions with Britvic and Bass, Speers joined Bottle Green Drinks in April 2002 because of the exciting growth opportunities in the adult soft drinks market. Bottle Green Drinks Co. is best known for its range of cordials and sparkling pressés for the adult palate, made using a unique cold filtration process.

Alan Sutton has enjoyed an association with the food service industry of over 30 years as a communicator, and is one of a small band of well-known contributors to its business-to-business magazines.

He spent several years as a staffer on *Caterer & Hotelkeeper*, where he held the positions of both Features Editor and Industrial Catering Editor, and continued to contribute regularly to the title, alongside other publications in the sector, until recently.

For the HCIMA he re-launched *Hospitality* magazine as a full colour publication and has edited other food service publications, including *Food Today* for Thomson Publishing and *Industrial Caterer* for Reed Publishing. Most recently he has worked for Dewberry Boyes, responsible for its titles *Pub Business* and *Quick Service Restaurant*.

Major food service businesses have retained him to produce their in-house publications, including Compass, Whitbread, Gleneagles Hotels, The Forum Hotel, Jersey Tourism and others.

Making it easy for your customers to pay

To attract new customers and provide them with as many ways to pay as possible, it's vital to accept credit and debit cards. Using plastic gives your customers more flexibility, and won't restrict them to the cash in their wallet or their cheque guarantee limit.

What's more, it involves minimum administration for your staff and can radically improve your cash flow. Of course, it will also allow you to tap into the potentially lucrative younger market for whom paying by plastic is an everyday occurrence.

An à la carte service from Barclaycard Merchant Services
Having decided to accept cards, you need to find the right service provider, or 'card acquirer' – one who can offer you the appropriate products and services for your business. For example, Barclaycard Merchant Services will talk to you in detail about your needs and plans and ensure that all your card processing requirements will be met.

Chips are good for you
Barclaycard Merchant Services can also help protect your business from fraudulent card use, by using the latest Chip and PIN technology. Chip and PIN, the nationwide initiative due to be introduced in 2005, will require cardholders to enter a Personal Identification Number (PIN) to authorise plastic card payments, rather than signing a receipt.

Serving up a choice of terminals
For this reason, the PDQ Portable from Barclaycard Merchant Services is particularly suitable for the hospitality sector, as it supports up to five mobile handsets within 50 metres of its base unit (depending on the environment and location). That means your customers can enter their PIN from the comfort of their table, helping you to avoid the risk of counterfeit card use.

Of course, Barclaycard Merchant Services also offers a range of other fast, compact, easy-to-use terminals for processing card payments, each of which is equipped with the latest anti-fraud technology.

Today's specials
Your individual card processing agreement with Barclaycard Merchant Services could also include a range of extra services or income-generating opportunities, such as:

- a 'gratuities function' that allows customers to add tips to their payments – and lets you control and distribute them as you wish
- E-Top Up, which lets you earn great levels of commission by topping up prepay mobile phones on your card processing terminal.

For more information
To find out how card processing could make your business more profitable, call Barclaycard Merchant Services on **0800 328 3299*** between 8.30am and 6pm, Monday to Friday.

*Calls may be monitored or recorded for training purposes.

> *"Barclaycard Merchant Services made it easy for me to accept payment by plastic. They talked me through a range of options and helped me find the right one for my business. Now my customers can choose how they want to pay – and don't rush off when their cash runs out."*
>
> Geoffrey Stockman, Director,
> Fingle Bridge Inn Ltd, Drewsteignton, Devon

Foreword

Welcome to *The Pubs, Bars and Clubs Handbook*, the new-look *Publican's Handbook*, which ran into five editions.

This year, with a new title, we take a new direction, making the pub, bar and club perform better. This isn't, however, another simple case of re-branding, with which anyone who runs a pub, bar or club will be all too familiar already. Rather, we are widening the scope of the publication in response to major changes in the nature of the licensed retail industry.

Perhaps the most noticeable change taking place right now is that split between the multiple-branded operations of pubs, bars, restaurants of all kinds and even clubs, and the remainder of the market. For, as one side becomes all the more strongly branded and ubiquitous (aren't all high streets starting to look the same?), so the remainder of the licensed retail market is converging.

What I mean by this is that pubs aren't what they were. Today's pub will be offering food of some sort, making it a little more like a restaurant. It may also offer quality accommodation, bringing it closer to a hotel. It may also do a big trade in premium packaged lagers (PPLs), alcopops or cocktails, taking it near to a club or cocktail bar – maybe even a wine bar. It might also be thriving as a pre-club venue.

Long gone are the days when a pub meant a pint and a pie (if you were lucky). There are precious few traditional pubs left, wet-led and setting their stall out to the wider community and to a not clearly defined target market. Talk to the operators of such and you'll meet with people who believe their days are numbered. Optimists are few.

What *is* happening in pubs, in everything from serving breakfasts (bringing them closer to cafes) and offering morning coffees and afternoon teas to tourists and shoppers (bringing them closer to tea rooms), is that those running successful operations are having to compete head on with all other sectors of the leisure

Peeks the Event Makers are proud to announce their Theme & Christmas Decorations Catalogues packed full of new ideas for the coming year. Peeks range of specially designed packs can now be ordered online 24 hours a day at **www.peeks.co.uk**

Peeks have put together a range of over 70 different theme packs designed to cater for any event – and with so much going on over the coming year, (as you will see from the diary of events listed at the front of their Theme catalogue) your spoilt for choice!

Peeks offer a full range of theme decorations to enhance any event. For easy to order theme packs to individual product, Peeks have a range of decorations to suit all occasions – specially designed for busy people.

For your food promotions Peeks Theme decorations will act as an eye-catching sales tool to attract customers, enhance your servery/bar area and encourage your customers to return. Dress it up with Peeks theme decorations and your customers will come back for more!

Christmas, as you will doubtless be all too aware, is a very important trading period in our calendar, and a season of great opportunity! With Peeks wide range of Christmas Crackers, Hats, Novelties & Decorations they offer the perfect mix of product to make the Christmas period a very festive (and profitable) time of year.

Their range of catering crackers are designed specially for the publican market and come in packs of 50 with a discount scale built in to bulk orders. Their hats and novelties (party poppers, rocket balloons, streamers, noisemakers & blowouts etc) really make the ideal finishing touch to any party or event.

Peeks have been in business for over 50 years and pride themselves on supplying quality products and excellent service at all times. They are always open to suggestions on their products and will, on request, produce specially designed packs (minimum order quantity 50) for Company Groups.

If requiring further details please contact them on **01202 489489**.

industry for a slice of the food and drink pound. And they are making an increasingly good fist of it too.

Similarly, restaurant-pubs, gastro-pubs, style bars, pre-club venues and all other parts of the market are having to learn from, and compete with, each other. There are many golden rules and instances of good retailing practice that are common to all and apply equally across the board.

And it is in response to this broadening of the bar trade that we have re-focused this publication. We trust that it appeals and applies just as much to the novice publican at a destination eatery as it does to the operator of a smart urban bar, where large measures of tequila and small portions of Mediterranean-style snacks are the order of the day. Alan Sutton's chapter on introducing a fast food and snacks trade, for example, can be picked up on by everyone with a bar operation. Bob Russell's chapter on presenting the business to attract passing trade also applies to every reader.

However, we aren't ditching tradition. Far from it, as we all know 'trad' is forever making a comeback. This year we have Ted Bruning of *What's Brewing* on the value of traditional beers, and Dominic Roskrow showing us how that most established of spirits, whisky, is making a strong comeback of its own – not least within style bars world-wide.

Our business is fast-changing. And *The Pubs, Bars and Clubs Handbook* will change with it, as always providing tips and ideas, approaches and strategies for the independent operator.

Danny Blyth
Consultant Editor

Part 1

Introduction

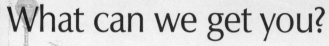
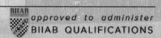

Tomorrow's Bar Business

John McNamara

Introduction

Since I walked through the doors of the Camberley offices of the British Institute of Innkeeping (BII) to take up the post of Chief Executive just over a year ago, my feet have hardly touched the ground. I have come to work within a professional organisation that is right at the heart of one of the most dynamic industries in the UK – the pub trade.

Over the last 10 years the hold of the big brewers has loosened and huge swathes of the market have been bought and sold, and re-sold. Within this rapid change lies the challenge for the modern licensee – and, to a certain extent, a Darwinian process of survival of the fittest has taken hold.

So how do you swim when others sink, and how do you ensure that your outlet is better than the other five on the same street? The answer lies in high-quality standards and professionalism. And with competition for the leisure pound ever-increasing, customers will vote with their feet if your standards are not up to scratch.

The pub has moved on from its smoky, male-dominated past, and the modern pub-goer has moved on with it. Females, families and over-50s are all significant markets for the modern pub trade, as is the 18–25-year-old age group, which has probably sparked the most major shifts in the trade over the past few years.

In the 1980s, the wine bar sprung up to cater for the so-called Yuppies, and over the next two decades this has evolved into the large stylish bar venues, branded chains and cocktail bars now present on almost every high street. These retail brands sparked a revolution for the pub industry that saw the customer become a lot more demanding and emphasised high standards.

By the early 1990s, taking on a pub was no longer something to consider for a comfortable retirement – it was, and remains today, a highly-demanding career for highly professional, multi-skilled business people.

Making the most of your business

Let's start with a quick quiz. What is the most important part of your business?

a) Your customers.
b) Your food and drink offer.
c) You and your staff.

If you didn't answer 'c) You and your staff', then it's your turn to sit in the corner with the white pointy hat on! Your establishment is only as good as the people who work there. Treat your staff right and you will build your customer base and boost your food and drink offer.

Top quality staff can light up a fairly dingy bar – but, equally, poor staff can drag down a quality outlet in a matter of days. And that goes for all your staff, from the most junior members of bar staff to the most senior manager – yes, that's you!

Training really is the key to this – and it must start the moment an employee begins to work for you. The first person the customer sees when they walk into your bar is a member of your staff – and, believe me, first impressions really do count. Training and keeping staff should be your priority.

The BII has worked over the last few years to provide a framework of qualifications that cover everything from the basic training of bar staff to a degree level diploma. It is important that staff are clear on what opportunities are out there for them and how they can reach their goals.

In the past there has been a serious lack of emphasis on investment in staff and this has left the trade with a very poor image among recruits and graduates. Like it or not, we are still seen as a part-time 'stop-gap' job, good enough for the college holidays but not taken seriously enough as a long-term career.

The resultant high staff turnover that this image problem has caused has, in its own right, contributed to the problem of high staff turnover – and so many licensees have been reluctant to invest in their staff for fear they will leave and the money will be wasted. But think about this for a minute. If every employer in the pub industry invested in training their staff and offered them career paths, perks, bonuses and incentives, there would be a ready-trained pool of professionals waiting to fill your next vacancy. After all, what goes around comes around!

And as any top licensee will tell you, that level of care and attention will always pay in the end, in all sorts of ways – in increased sales and customer satisfaction, for example, not simply length of service. And a happy employee is apt to return to you periodically throughout their career.

Social responsibilities

Having established that your staff are the face of your business, it is also important to equip them for the task. Apart from issues of customer service standards and quality, the government has been taking a long, hard look at the licensing laws recently, in conjunction with the BII and other trade organisations, and we are expecting a new licensing bill to receive Royal assent this summer.

As with the Criminal Justice and Police Act and the Licensing (Young Persons) Act, the onus under the reforms is on you and your staff to help fight underage drinking and alcohol-related violence and to protect the public, especially young people, from harm. Failure to take your social responsibilities seriously enough won't just harm your business, it could land you in trouble with the law and, ultimately, if you haven't put in place the proper training, you leave yourself open to prosecution and could lose your licence and your livelihood. In other words, if your new member of bar staff is let loose without training and serves an underage drinker on her first night in the job, then both she and you, the licensee, carry the can.

In light of the increasing importance of this side of the trade, the BII has launched its own social responsibilities initiative aimed at tackling these and other issues. This encourages licensees to sign up to local initiatives like Pubwatch, which help to exclude known trouble-makers from pubs and bars in an area.

The BII also supports the new PASS scheme, which provides holograms for proof-of-age cards to help weed out fakes, and also backs organisations like The Portman Group, which seeks to ensure drinks marketing is sensible and does not encourage irresponsible or underage drinking.

But what do the customers want?

Think back to your last visit to someone else's pub. What was it that made or destroyed the visit? It's odds on that some really small detail made all the difference – and it is these little touches that count. For example, using branded glassware can make a difference – it is things like having a different glass for a different product that the customer will, consciously or even sub-consciously, pick up on. Is the bar clean? Are the empties cleared off the tables regularly? Are the ashtrays full? Is it smoky? Are the toilets clean? These are the things that can make or break your pub.

Staff should be trained to maintain the environment in the pub to a high standard so that it is clean and welcoming. And you should never assume you know what your customers want.

Ask them

Comment cards, loyalty programmes, mystery visits and spot checks all help build a picture of how your standards shape up. And even a customer complaint can be turned around by a good operator and turned into a positive if it's acted on.

Upholding professionalism

So, I return to the issue of professionalism, which is at the heart of everything we at the BII do. We represent over 15,000 members across the UK and embrace everyone from students to very experienced licensees within the trade.

The comprehensive framework of qualifications we offer has helped take the job of licensee to a level where it has status, and we aim to continue building on this by growing our membership, offering more benefits to our members and increasing our portfolio of qualifications.

As a professional body we are also able to represent our members at the highest level of government and the regulatory system, giving this very important sector a voice that it has lacked in the past. Add to this professional dimension the package of business building and cost reducing benefits, and membership represents outstanding value.

Conclusion

And finally, the pub trade is too diverse to summarise in such a short space but the key themes that run through it are clear: professionalism, training and quality. If you aim for, and achieve, high standards in these areas you are well on your way to succeeding. And the key lies in constant innovation. The best in the business are rarely to be seen twiddling their thumbs in the office if they could be behind the bar motivating their key asset – their staff!

The British Institute of Innkeeping's awarding body, BIIAB, offers a wide range of qualifications for the industry, from barstaff, licence application through to career development.

These widely recognised qualifications are highly relevant and respond to the needs of pub and bar operators within today's marketplace. Whether for starters joining the industry, or for experienced personnel, there is an appropriate solution within the BIIAB qualifications portfolio. Our promise is jargon-free, practical solutions that can be applied in the workplace.

The BII is committed to making its qualifications highly accessible and delivered to excellent standards. BIIAB has over 330 approved centres through colleges, private training providers and retail companies all over the UK.

By meeting the national criteria of the Qualifications and Curriculum Authority (QCA), BIIAB qualifications have gained additional status by being part of the national framework. Qualifications in the national framework may be eligible for public funding.

As a result of QCA accreditation some of our qualifications have had a title change. This has been necessary to meet standardisation processes at QCA. The syllabus content and the assessment of these qualifications remain exactly the same as before.

A Quick Guide to What's Available

Qualifications for Licensing

Handbooks for all the qualifications for licensing are available by calling the BII on 01276 684449 or e-mail reception@bii.org.

BIIAB Level 2 National Certificate for Licensees (NCL) (formerly National Licensee's Certificate) and Scottish Licensee's Certificate (SLC)

The NCL, available for On-, Off- and Part IV licences, gives prospective licensees knowledge of basic licensing law and the social responsibilities attached to the retail sale of alcohol. It has become a virtual 'must-have' for licence applications and is widely available through BIIAB approved centres such as pub operating companies, Further & Higher Education Colleges, some universities and independent training providers.

The Scottish Licensee's Certificate (Off-Sale and all other licences) caters for the differences in law for Scotland and is accessible through BIIAB approved centres.

BIIAB Level 2 National Certificate for Door Supervisors – Licensed Premises (NCDS) (formerly Door Supervisor's National Certificate)

The NCDS provides door supervisors with the knowledge and skills required to do the job professionally. The additional modules can be accredited individually on the

NCDS 'passport'. NCDS is a knowledge-based qualification which encompasses licensing law, health and safety regulations, arrest procedures and a variety of other topics. Additional modules include skills training in first aid, conflict management and physical interventions. The NCDS is available through BIIAB approved centres in collaboration with City & Guilds and the Hospitality Awarding Body.

BIIAB Level 2 National Certificate for Entertainment Licensees (NCEL) (formerly Entertainment Licensee's National Certificate)

The NCEL is designed to help managers and licensees comply with a wide range of safety requirements, attain understanding of entertainment licensing law and the social responsibilities attached to running venues with a Public Entertainment Licence. The NCEL is available through BIIAB approved centres in collaboration with City & Guilds and the Hospitality Awarding Body.

BIIAB Level 2 National Certificate for Licensees (Drugs Awareness) (NCL(DA)) (formerly Licensee's National Drugs Certificate)

The NCL(DA) provides licensees and managers of all types of licensed premises, from the small country pub to the inner city club venue, with an awareness of the illegal drugs scene. It provides operational guidelines to help prevent drug problems arising and also tactics to enable licensees to deal with such problems, should they arise. The NCL(DA) is available through BIIAB approved centres in collaboration with City & Guilds and the Hospitality Awarding Body.

Qualifications for Management Induction

The BIIAB offers two qualifications for management induction, the BIIAB Level 2 National Certificate in Licensed Retailing (NCLR) and the Induction Examination Certificate (IC). Both incorporate the NCL (On) or SLC and each cover the core skills for people new to the industry. The NCLR and IC are widely used as induction qualifications by both managed and non-managed operators. The IC is available through BIIAB approved centres such as pub operating companies, independent training providers and further education colleges while the NCLR is available through Further Education Colleges and independent training providers.

Qualifications for Staff Development

The Barperson's National Certificate (BNC)

The BNC is designed to equip the barperson with a clear understanding of licensing law as it applies to people working behind the bar. It delivers clear statements of the law and the responsibilities associated with serving alcoholic drinks, underage customers and dealing with difficulties. Knowledge is tested using a telephone assessment procedure and the qualification can be studied for, and taken on licensed premises.

The Professional Barperson's Qualification (PBQ)

Intended to help licensees develop more senior staff, the PBQ is designed to develop skills to respond to a rapidly changing and competitive market environment. Delivered in-house, the qualification comprises two units:

1 Barperson's National Certificate (telephone based assessment as stated overleaf)
2 Customer and Drinks Service (based on written assessment)

Qualifications for Management Development

This suite of nine Advanced Qualifications (AQs) has been developed to deliver commercial benefits in specific areas. They enable licensed retailers to respond to competitive demands and to develop a highly motivated team. BIIAB approved centres have experienced staff to ensure consistently high standards of delivery. Each AQ is designed to suit managers, tenants/lessees, business development and area managers and is highly focused to encourage participants to implement ideas in the workplace.

Licensed Retail Business Development Certificate

Designed to give licensees the ability to challenge their whole business plan in the context of a competitive market and their current trade.

Licensed Retail Catering Management Certificate

Helps licensees capitalise on the growing market for good pub food by providing the knowledge to help set up and manage a pub catering operation.

Cellar & Beer Quality Management Certificate

Informs licensees how to ensure their beer is consistently served in optimum condition, to increase sales and to decrease wastage.

Customer Service Management Certificate

Gives licensees the inspiration, ideas and ability to manage excellent customer service to increase repeat business and attract new customers.

Licensed Retail Financial Management Certificate

Includes practical knowledge of basic accounting practices and terminology, enabling licensees to understand the financial structure and control of their business.

Leadership & Motivation Certificate

Enables licensees to improve staff performance and team performance through effective leadership and motivation.

Licensed Retail Practical Trainer Certificate

Shows licensees how to deliver highly practical training programmes, which fit into normal working practice and shifts, as well as producing improvements in business performance.

Spirit Retail Certificate

Designed to help licensees improve marketing, merchandising and presentation of spirits and to grow spirit sales without affecting other products.

Wine Retail Certificate

Helps licensees capitalise on the growing demand for wine in pubs, bars and restaurants and to increase sales and profit by merchandising, upselling and serving wine effectively.

Advanced Qualifications Diploma in Licensed Retailing

The AQ Diploma consolidates the different assignments completed by candidates for each of five AQ certificates into a coherent portfolio. In addition, it requires that candidates put the key components of each AQ into practice in their business and then monitor the impact that this has on the business performance. To be awarded the AQ Diploma candidates must demonstrate that they have implemented the business ideas, from the certificates they already hold, in their outlets.

For further information about the syllabuses of Institute qualifications, please contact:
Qualifications Department
The British Institute of Innkeeping
Wessex House
80 Park Street
Camberley, Surrey
GU15 3PT
Tel: 01276 684449
Fax: 01276 23045
E-mail: qualifications@bii.org
Website: www.bii.org

To apply for centre approval for your organisation, or for a current list of approved centres, please contact:
Quality Assurance Department
BIIAB
Wessex House
80 Park Street
Camberley, Surrey
GU15 3PT
Tel: 01276 684449
Fax: 01276 23045
E-mail: awards@bii.org
Website: www.bii.org

2

Business Opportunities

Danny Blyth

Though trading conditions for 2003 are set to stay challenging, there remains as much scope for the go-ahead independent operator of a pub, bar or club as there has been for a long while.

First, there is the now established advantage in your trading position (versus the multiple-branded operations) of your ability to effect changes promptly, without need of committees. If a demand rockets for a style of service, or for a certain brand of drink or flavour of food, then you can go some way towards meeting it, just as soon as you can get organised.

Following on, you have your own unique identity to trade on. You have the ability to make a real and personal difference to what goes on.

All this sets you apart from the opposition and remains the strength of the independent. However, in this fast-changing market there are several business opportunities for the independent that seem to be growing. Here are just four.

Licensing hours

We can safely bet that, when the entire UK is finally granted the chance of extended and more flexible opening hours, the big high street names will be first to the post and stretch every last penny from longer available trading times.

I'm sure some of the big boys will do well, but equally sure that retail standards will come under pressure, first in terms of simple things like general levels of cleanliness and orderliness. Overheads will prove a problem, especially if a chain remains open simply because it doesn't wish to lose any trade a to nearby rival chasing the same customer group.

First Class business opportunities and leading edge support

At Greene King Pub Partners our reputation precedes us. With a diverse estate of 1,082 pubs throughout the South of England ranging from community locals to multi-bedroom hotels and winners of the Publican Awards, leased and tenanted Pub Company of the Year 2001, 2002 and 2003, we know we've got a lot to shout about.

We're not about short term profit and returns, we're a long term player, which has allowed a focused approach of building for the future through a continued programme of property maintenance, developments, business support and most importantly a sound relationship with licensees.

Recruiting and Retaining the very best...

There is a choice of tenancy and lease agreements to ensure licensees can fully develop their business objectives coupled with an extensive training and development programme to ensure that licensees have the right skills to create and build a sustainable business

Sustainable Growth in Sales...

To help develop and grow the business we have an extensive support and incentive programme which includes a full demographic, categorisation and marketing research profile of the outlet plus an incentive programme to reward licensees for growth in sales, annual promotion plan, fantastic product portfolio including "Time for Wine" support package, a unique Buying Guide and off the shelf and seasonal promotion campaigns targeted at specific categories of outlets.

Creating Customer Loyalty…

We have a selection of loyalty promotions, which bring customers together and give licensees the chance to thank them for their business. This year, 545 licensees and 7,618 of their customers joined them at the races and many others went golfing and fishing creating a great avenue to build customer loyalty.

Developing a Strong Estate…

Our maintenance programme ensures our buildings are kept to a very high standard and with the £16 million invested last year and a further £10.2 million for this year has ensured we've developed a strong estate, with state of the art facilities for both our present and our future licensees to tempt in customers.

One thing's for sure at Greene King Pub Partners, licensees have got the support to take their business from strength to strength.

Tradition with a TWIST

There's more to Greene King than meets the eye. Because while we take pride in the traditional pub – and with a history going back 200 years, who on earth can blame us – we're still able to offer you a truly refreshing change. With more than 1,100 pubs with a mixture of tenancies and leases, you can be sure we will find the right opportunities for you.

When we say partnership, for example, we mean it. Comprehensive training. Practical advice to help you get the most out of your business. A commitment to maintaining high-quality premises. It all adds up to full support wherever, whenever you need it. Which, of course, makes running your very own pub all the more rewarding. Please visit our website or call our recruitment line on 01284 714497.

GREENE KING
17 99
FINE ALES

And, of course, the poor managers will be flogged to death. In many a chain now, managers are over-worked and rarely seen interacting with customers, far less having the time to be actually policing standards out on the floor.

The opportunity is there for independent operators to use wider possible opening hours wisely. To open when trade is there and close when it cannot be had is simplicity itself, but that option won't be available to many a manager at a branded pub, bar or eatery.

And if the independent can maintain high retail standards during all hours of opening, then, again, he'll as likely steal a march on the big brands. Then there is that 'people' issue of yourself and the difference you can make. If you are out there, open and working when you choose, you're likely to be fresher and sharper, and so too will the rest of your staff.

Finally, as and when opening times are reformed, the opportunity to set up a different style of bar will apply just as much to the independent as it does to the big groups. Whether you fancy being more of a pre-club venue or something even more like a late-night venue proper, you can develop a unique concept for yourself. Likely reforms to end limits on numbers of live performers also open up further opportunities.

Middle-aged appeal

It's a rare week when the news, trade or broadcast media doesn't carry news of a major piece of research that shows where most of the UK's disposable income is held – in the purses and wallets of the over-50s.

Some surveys show that up to 60 per cent of the nation's readies are held by the middle-aged. And no wonder – many of the group are 'empty nesters', what with the family grown up and gone from the nest. Some have their mortgages paid off and others are early retired – perhaps the last generation ever that will have benefited from final salary pension agreements.

With such a bounty out there it's perhaps surprising that the multiple operators remain so youth-focused. Save for a handful of food-led, usually semi-rural pub brands, they haven't made much of a play for the middle-aged pound.

I feel that the independent operator can do better with this age group. First, assuming your pub or bar has a fair degree of 'community feel' or inclusiveness, you have a strong base to build on already. A common gripe among these people is that when it comes to going out for a drink or a meal these days they are excluded. They are made to 'feel old'.

Following on, the key, perhaps, is not to concentrate the business into a social club for those who've only recently taken up golf or motorcycling. After all, these people have grown up more independently and can even remember a time when the UK was near free of branded operations. It's a tricky thing, but a strong appeal to their core need for a place that is marked by being welcoming, clean, and free of bad behaviour and language will go a long way. Consistently high standards of food and drink will seal the deal.

Sure, you can pamper the middle-aged by little things like training staff to make a show of filling the water jug with fresh water and presenting it alongside a malt whisky; but perhaps just as important is a *lack* of certain things that these people regard as a huge turn-off. Top of the list here are bar staff who aren't welcoming and friendly and haven't a word to say to anyone who isn't their own age. Or staff who need music – loud music or their type of music – on permanently, to their pleasure and the customer's pain.

Once levels of inclusivity have been enhanced and a regular middle-aged following is building, more ambitious moves might be attempted. Promotions and theme nights, for instance, could be run around winter ales or malt whiskies, instead of DJs and alcopops. The middle-aged like a party too. After all, they go back as far as rock and roll itself.

Going canny?

Readers should remember that this is a Scot writing. There is a terrible problem in this country of mean handedness in the trade. We're all under pressure to control costs and to conform to the wishes (increasingly demands) of the bean counters – but must things be so tight?

What I'm suggesting here is that a little more generosity from the independent bar operator can go a long way. At my own favourite pub (a highly unusual affair, being a metropolitan-style modern bar and restaurant stuck in a rural village) pre-dinner G&Ts are a treat. Measures are a little bigger than they ought to be and we get as much tonic as we like. Price is higher than usual but the perception of value is infinitely above that offered by big chains (where, incidentally, the bean counting can extend to how many slivers of lemon must be cut from each fruit!). Being offered a choice on top of the market leader Gordon's, including premiums like Tanquarray and Bombay Sapphire, inspires – again, something that's rare in the multiples with their strong tied agreements. But being served with a flourish (getting top quality ice, a choice of lemon or lime, and 'top-notch' glassware) and getting a perfect serve time after time makes this leasehold pub as good as the Ritz.

Elsewhere, I do wish I had the proverbial fiver for every time I've seen a customer crestfallen after ordering G&T at a bar – including well-run independently-owned premises. It seems that skimping is *de rigueur*, and not just with this classic old mixed drink. A little slackening of the reins might go a long way to building goodwill, and this is yet again one little area where the independent trader can make his mark.

Personality plus

Finally, the independent trader is, put simply, often a lot more fun. Whether it's a pub, bar, food-led operation or more of a club-type environment, I always seem to find more character in the place if there is a proprietor and not a manager.

Customers love not just the familiar face, but somebody who 'takes ownership' for real, and with whom the buck stops should a complaint need to be made. Ask yourself, if Bogart had been a unit manager at Rick's in *Casablanca*, would he really have risked hiding those transit papers in Sam's piano? Would Laszlo have been served at the bar? Of course Major Strasse and his henchmen might have been barred because of their insistence of wearing their working clothes. Claude Rains shone as a dodgy Vichy officer but would have paled as an M&S besuitted Area Manager (though there are parallels here!).

Individuality is a strength to trade on, particularly in a world where character is increasingly giving way to conformity and the homogeneous. If anything, the trade needs more eccentricity and individualism. So please, be bold, be big and brash if it suits. Be yourself. We're all the better for that.

Part 2

Improving profitability on drinks

Trouble-free, safer drinks dispense

By BOC Sureflow, the cellar management experts

The success of your business depends on how well you serve your customers. That means you need a reliable source of top quality gases for drinks dispense . Whatever type of bar you operate, and whether you count your customers in dozens or thousands, you'll need a gas supplier that has the expertise, experience and resources to provide the highest standards of quality and service.

Gas supply you can rely on

A lack of gas when you need it, will interfere with your routine and empty cylinders can clutter the cellar causing a safety hazard to normal operations. Storing more gas cylinders in the cellar is *not* the best solution, as this increases safety risks and means you could end up paying more for your gas supply.

BOC Sureflow's practical and economic solution to continuous gas supply is the milkround gas delivery, which means just the right amount of gas is delivered at regular, agreed intervals. So bar staff can get on with the business of serving customers, safe in the knowledge that cylinders will automatically arrive with the next milkround delivery.

BOC Sureflow's local Sales Service Personnel deliver the gas and are trained experts in gas dispense management. Making life easier for bar staff, because the Sales Service Person will connect cylinders, remove empties, check for leaks and manage cylinder stocks for you. So you can say goodbye to problems in the cellar knowing that your gas dispensing needs are in safe, capable hands.

Technology you can depend on

New gas dispense technologies, particularly those using larger cylinders, are ideal for licensed outlets. These systems can help to dispense beer or soft drinks at a faster rate, reduce fobbing and save time by removing the hassle of changing over cylinders.

BOC Sureflow leads the way in developing dispense equipment that uses less cylinders and is more reliable and safer to operate. Licensees all over the country are now switching to SureBlend and Cellasure mixed gas dispense systems and benefiting from improved product quality and savings.

Quality you can count on

One gas cylinder may look very much like another, but don't be fooled by a freshly branded cylinder. Some unscrupulous dealers will acquire and brand stolen cylinders and whilst the exterior appears OK, the interior may be severely corroded and in a dangerous condition. This presents a high safety risk to staff and the corrosion will contaminate drinks producing an unpleasant metallic taste.

Your customers demand a perfect pint and soft drinks experience. If they don't get the quality they expect they will look elsewhere. BOC Sureflow operates to ISO 9001-2000 International quality standards. Its high quality food grade dispense gases, and purity of gas mixtures, ensures perfect beverage taste and presentation – time after time.

Safety you can trust

With the increase in cellar gas volumes in recent years, licensees now find themselves handling a lot more CO_2 and mixed gas and facing more safety issues and legal responsibilities to protect staff.

Anyone who doesn't assess the risks associated with dispense gases could be putting themselves and their business in danger. BOC Sureflow has a well-earned reputation as the industry's safety experts. As well as providing safety information, BOC Sureflow has developed a range of innovative and low cost risk assessment and safety training packages to help you comply with current health and safety regulations.

To find out more:

Visit us online at:
www.bocsureflow.co.uk
where *FREE* registration gives you access to essential gas and safety information.

Call our customer centre on:
08457 302 302
Available 24 hours a day, 7 days a week.

3

Selling and Promotions

Danny Blyth

The fast-moving licensed retail industry is producing a new type of entrepreneur. He or she is bolder, thinks bigger and has a lot to offer in the way of inspiration. This modern operator is in stark contrast to those who have gone before. In former times conditions were, in many ways, much easier for the entire trade, and the bar operators could survive happily without a well-developed strategy for selling and promotion. Customers used to drink at lunchtimes and often return to the premises for more drink on the way home. Drinking was a much more accepted part of culture and nobody had to struggle all that much for business.

Things could not be more different today. Drinking is frowned upon during the working day – if not outlawed – and, indeed, in some corporate circles it's following smoking as becoming altogether undesirable. Then there is increased competition, both from within the bar business itself and between the trade and an ever-widening leisure industry.

As the financial and operational climate has moved on so too have the demands for effective selling and promotion. The pub industry of old would see the occasional quirky little promotion dreamt up by either a recent college graduate or, more likely, a next-to-useless member of the controlling family who'd been moved as far sideways as possible short of the labour exchange – that is, into marketing. But today there are infinitely slicker promotions being run by big brands and retail groups. And the plain truth for the independent operator is that he's up against it from all sides.

Hence the emergence of a more focused bar operator, in many cases more pushy and aggressive in his approach but certainly more effective. There's no great rocket science here, just a series of operational tools that add up to a winning strategy. Here is a brief look at some of those areas where taking a more radical line can make a difference.

Timing promotions

Received wisdom in the industry has it that drinks promotions must be concentrated upon those drinks with the higher GPs – and that the offer runs when the premises are at their most full, at peak time in the evenings. This does make good sense. After all, the last thing you need is somebody coming up with a whizz of an idea to double your sales of Benedictine, whereas doubling your volume of Stella really would be mouth watering. And, of course, a 100 per cent uptake of an offer is of little use when the place is near empty.

The only trouble is that premises are open for much longer than the peak evening session, and outside of this time in many bars, and certainly most pubs, the greatest sellers are usually the standard lagers and bitters and not the premiums.

One of the more innovative lines I've seen of late is to promote those top selling standard draught beers along with a meal as a part of a fixed price lunchtime promotion. Lunchtimes have, until late, been quite free of drinks promotions but remain an area of opportunity. Building on the dry lunchtime company culture, lunchtimes can also be used to promote soft drinks, either in price promotions that encourage upsizing or else as part of lunchtime meal deals (just as they are with many a high street quick-service catering outlet).

Following on, breakfasts and brunches offer further scope for offers and promotions, as do morning coffees and afternoon teas (even a simple Danish with the coffee or scone with the tea offers upselling possibilities).

These are just some of the ideas being put into practice by enterprising independents.

Big brand time

Nevertheless, big brands – of everything from ready-to-drinks (RTDs), through premium packaged lagers (PPLs), and on to spirits – do have a major place on the promotions calendar. They are the big sellers, they usually offer a good GP, and any activity they offer is usually accompanied by high-quality props in the way of merchandiser and point-of-sale (POS) materials. And if it's prizes they're offering, to either end-customers or trade incentives, it will be on the lines of a week in Australia and not Anglesey.

A lot of operators will do what's expected of them in terms of taking part in a trade promotion, using the POS, making the offer and, hopefully, seeing something positive out of it. However, I'm noting an increasing amount of independents going a stage further and, in consequence, doing much better out of the exercise.

For instance, some people are building on to the brand promotion – customising it, if you prefer. This involves house-manufactured blackboarding and external signs to complement what comes in from the supplier. It means taking some time to add extra elements to any promotion, thereby increasing its chances of success and, along the way, adding value for the supplier.

One licensee I know in Wimbledon regularly adds to any prize element by offering his own range of winnable goodies – this guarantees that at least some customers who come along on the night will go away with something, and this is much better than everyone going home having filled in a postcard in the hope of scooping that dream holiday.

This particular operator has much to offer. He won't jump at every brand promotion that comes along, only those that he is convinced both suit his style of operation and fit in with his business goals. Over a long time he's built up a reputation among suppliers, who have come to expect that if he takes part, increased volumes will follow. This is a crucial part of the relationship, especially for younger operators new to promotions – a supplier must be confident in your ability to deliver if he's to allow himself to be squeezed more than he'd like in terms of discounts, cost free stock or whatever. Only once you've reached this stage can you go one better again – like our man in Wimbledon – and take your enhanced promotional plans to a supplier and say: 'Here's the details and here's how much it will cost for me to take part.'

While this might appear a bit too brash for some, remember that nothing motivates a supplier as much as increased volumes. Take them a firm promotional plan with that main aim and you're on the way. If you are a multiple licensee then you are on an even stronger bet.

Smaller brands

The independent operator is also increasingly innovative with new and lesser known brands. And, as an independent, you can react much quicker to any new fad or taste than most managers – especially in the fast moving and fickle areas of flavoured alcoholic beverages (FABs) and premium packaged spirits (PPSs). You can get a small quantity of something in fast and see how customers react. A manager must wait for the prescribed list to be altered. By the same token, you can pick up on how many independents are making the most from things like shooters and cocktails by making up your own menu and, say, offering them by waitress service at tables.

This versatility isn't lost on even the most traditional pub. Many an independent has worked with a local microbrewer to badge a beer as a house beer, using the name of the pub on the pump clip. Others run offbeat beer festivals – not just for winter warmers or milds in the month of May, but also for summer ales or ales with wacky names or with sporting links. The important thing is to be individual. That often comes with being innovative.

Staff sell

The human side to the trade remains vitally important, not just in selling during promotions but at all times. Customers continue to value good service from a warm welcome through to a fond farewell. And it's in this personal side of things that I'm seeing many instances of good practice among independent operators.

In the first place there are independents operating a system of training and appraisal for bar staff every bit as good as the big multiple operators. A good starting point for this is getting hold of a copy of what the big players are up to (not difficult if you are friends with a local manager). In developing your own plan and working in your own set of retail standards there is professional help available through bodies such as the British Institute of Innkeeping (BII) – and just because there's an 'Innkeeping' in that title doesn't mean the expertise isn't just as applicable to a late licensed venue (LLV), or a food-led or more modern bar operation.

Second, what I notice most about the successful independent when it comes to selling and promotion is that staff are 'on board' at all times. There are clear standards and clear goals for sure, but put into practice in an altogether more personal fashion than the 'brand values' of the big chains. This is a great comparative strength to trade on. Just as you as an individual are free to stamp your own personality on the business, be it through sheer enthusiasm or perhaps a more laid-back approach (or even through misbehaving!), assembling a staff around you to complement your style helps set your offer apart from the multiples.

Selling and promoting yourself and your offer is, after all, the most important sale to be made.

4

The Youth Market

Dominic Roskrow

If you're thinking about making a positive move to attract the youth market, then you might want to take the advice of one leading pub company Chief Executive. When asked for one piece of advice he smiled and said: 'Don't bother.' And if you're determined to press ahead anyway, then the next piece of advice is: 'Do so, but with extreme caution.'

Successfully ensnaring the youth market is the holy grail of the drinks trade. The under-35s are young, free and often single; they tend to have a high level of disposable income; they tend to go out more and stay out longer; and they're very brand aware. More than that, they're prepared to invest substantial sums of money paying top prices to make sure they're in the right environment and that they're seen with the right product.

But catching the youth market is like surfing: you have to pick your moment, ride the fashion wave for as long as you can stay on it, then get off, start again and try and pick the next roller-coaster.

It's not only a difficult market to get to grips with, it's a fickle and fast-changing one, and it is ruthless and unforgiving. Get your offering wrong and you could drive any regular clientele you had away and have nothing to replace it with. And even if you get it right, you will eventually have to make a stark choice between evolving your outlet to keep hold of the youth you have as they grow older, or abandoning them for the next generation of party-goers.

For the simple fact remains: one person's trendy haunt is his younger brother's idea of an old fogies' bar. The chances are you are going to struggle to be all things to everybody. But there are ways that different markets can co-exist in your pub.

In essence this means clearly segregating time within your venue and advertising the fact that you are doing so.

If you decide, for instance, that every Thursday, Friday and Saturday night will be aimed at the 18–30-year-old market, you must advertise that fact well to both older customers and younger ones. You need a clear point at which the evening changes, and an hour before that time arrives the music should be taken up a notch and made more lively, and the lighting adjusted accordingly.

This will subtly encourage the daytime clientele to leave the pub without being made to feel unwelcome. None of this is easy and takes a great deal of time and effort.

If you do decide to go ahead with it anyway, then there are plenty of positive reasons why you might want to do so beyond the financial. Vibrant, lively and youthful venues are fun places to be, they create a momentum of their own, and they allow the operator to be flamboyant and experimental. Hard work – but fun hard work.

Research your subject

Before you do anything, research your subject carefully. Visit bars in your area and take note of what they're stocking; compile a list of opposition outlets, and note any unusual features or points of difference they have.

Seek advice from as many different sources as you possibly can. Talk to all your drinks suppliers about popular brands and make sure you stock them. Consider commissioning a street survey, and ask youngsters where they go out and why they go there.

Stock the right brands

It's not hard to find out the brands young drinkers want most, and 80 per cent of your stock will stay fairly constant. Brands such as Stella, Kronenbourg, Beck's etc have reached icon status and are unlikely to fall by the wayside on the whim of fashion. But being prepared to stock new brands and fad brands and react quickly when the trends move on is very important.

Get the music right

Don't make the mistake of thinking you can do this for yourself. Music is probably the most important single factor when getting a young persons' venue right, and the hardest to do well.

The best way of getting this right is to bring in outside help. Find who the trendiest DJs are and talk to them about hosting club nights in the pub and advising on other nights. The modern DJ will have his own following, and although it will cost you to use him, you'll guarantee an audience and he'll be able to provide you with instant credibility.

You will be able to negotiate all sorts of deals. Allow him to advertise his gigs through fly posters and he'll undoubtedly repay the compliment.

Embrace technology

Without getting too insulting about it, today's youngsters have the attention span of a gnat and demand to be entertained constantly. Music isn't enough. The more television screens or video walls you have, the better. Internet and quiz machines are all but essential, and on-screen promotions will go down particularly well.

Technology is most appreciated among youngsters when it is being used for promotional purposes. Telephone texting is one of the best ways to involve customers and to drive trade.

A number of texting companies are in the market place and will be able to do everything from just informing customers of a special drinks offer to linking up customers for playing quizzes or even pub-dating.

You can build a comprehensive database from the information that customers submit and can use it to send text messages offering anything from a free birthday drink to information on your next major event.

In one case a pub offered a text voucher to customers – all the recipient had to do was go to the bar at a certain time and show the text message to get a free drink. It brought in 65 extra customers on a Monday night. Drinks suppliers promoting a new product will only be too happy to help with such a promotion.

Get the food offering right

Go for simple snack style foods such as wraps, burgers, nachos and so on. And try to offer something easy but a bit different. One pub in the south west has started offering omelettes with a variety of sweet and savoury toppings. At weekends that's all they offer – and they have seen food turnover rocket.

Have high-profile promotions

Encourage tasting nights, get the drinks companies bringing in new products and, where you get the chance, make sure your pub is used for key competitions or promotions around big sporting events. If you can attract in the major drinks companies they will do much of the hard work for you by providing people to give out the drinks and the promotional material to make sure the event is a success.

Attract women

Offer bottles of wine or Bacardi Breezers at half price before a certain time, or hold an event aimed at women. The fact remains that, even in this day and age, groups of women will attract groups of men. Making your pub female-friendly is therefore essential.

Consider gimmicks

Tacky as it might be, many of them work. Fancy condom machines, a good selection of cigarettes, a bottles-only serving hatch and spirits dispensed manually are all easy and effective ways of adding a touch extra to your pub offering.

Listen to your customers

Ask your customers either directly or indirectly what they want from the pub and what they would like to see you offer. In this way they will feel that they have an ownership stake in the pub.

Remember the basics

Perhaps most importantly of all, remember what type of pub you are and don't lose sight of that. One of the advantages you have over your opposition is that you are a pub, and often many of the more traditional aspects of your establishment placed alongside a new one are what makes it so attractive. Cask ale, for instance, can enjoy a healthy following among younger drinkers.

The youth market is always looking for somewhere else to go and something new to do. The skill of catering for that market is reinventing yourself so that they constantly feel there is something new about your offering.

It's a tough nut to crack, but with enough foresight, hard work and planning, the 18–35-year-old market can be catered for, and the benefits are massive.

But remember – know your limits and never stop surfing.

5

Beer with Class

Ted Bruning

The challenge for tomorrow's winning bar operator is to make your beer offer exciting – and to keep it that way. For the trouble with beer is, they've let it get boring. It's not sexy any more. It's not classy any more. It's no fun.

That's why fewer and fewer people want it. That's why less and less of it is being sold and why more and more people are turning to flavoured alcoholic beverages (FABs) and premium-packaged spirits (PPSs) and ready-to-drinks (RTDs) and what have you. Though it's still a sizeable part of turnover, for many it could do better. It's time the industry did something to put the sparkle back into beer.

It's not that beer hasn't been properly marketed over the years. British brewers and suppliers spend the GNP of a small African country on marketing and advertising every year, and the 'Cream of Manchester' and 'Smoothly Does It' ads are some of the cleverest, wittiest and best produced on TV.

If anything, the problem is that the big brands have been *over*-marketed and *over*-distributed. Wherever you go, it's the same damn thing – Tetley, John Smith's, Boddingtons, Carling, Carlsberg, Stella, Kronenbourg. In almost every bar in every high street in every town you go to, you see the same handful of brands. Not that the leading brands aren't fine products in their own right, but it's as if BHS, Debenhams and M&S were the only department stores left, and you either wore what they sold or went naked.

But what consumers – especially, but not only, the free-spending younger consumers – really crave is excitement; variety – novelty, if you like. And where is all the excitement and variety and novelty in the drinks market right now? It's in FABs. It's in PPSs and RTDs. It's in cream liqueurs.

If the beer market wants to get moving again, the big players need to shake off their addiction to megabrands – and so, too, do those who run our pubs and bars.

The Stellas and Boddingtons of this world may be safe bets from the vantage point of the Interbrew boardroom. But from the consumer's point of view, safety is among the least desirable of characteristics. We don't go out to have a safe time. We go out to have a wild time. Safe bets equal reliable. Safe bets equal dull. Safe bets aren't sexy.

The strategy of most big brewers for the past few years has been to increase the market share of their leading brands. Ironically, the very opposite is true in the retail trade. Nobody's trying to swamp the world with All Bar Ones or Pitcher & Pianos or Slug & Lettuces. What they're trying to do is tailor their brands very closely to their perceived market niches. You wouldn't expect to find an It's a Scream in a country village, for instance, or a Harvester in a city centre. But a brewery would actively seek to stock the same leading beer brands in an It's a Scream, in a Harvester and in a village local. One size, in short, fits all.

The market, however, doesn't agree. It's notoriously difficult to gauge actual demand in the British beer market, thanks to the distorting effect of the tie. Just because everybody's *got* John Smith's, for instance, doesn't mean everybody *wants* John Smith's. What it means is that the people behind John Smith's have an awful lot of power and can make sure that John Smith's, and nothing but John Smith's, is on every bar whether consumers really want it or not.

The tie makes it very difficult for the trade and consumers to express their genuine demand; but there is one cast-iron test of whether genuine demand is actually being met or not. If consumers are faced with liking it or lumping it, they lump it. All they can do is vote with their feet and either stay home with a few bottles of premium bottled ale from the supermarket or opt out of beer altogether and drink FABs and PPSs instead. Both of which they are doing, in droves.

So how to make your own beer offer sexy? Take a look in the least likely direction imaginable – the real ale market. Now there's nothing obviously sexy about real ale – or about the people who drink it, for that matter. The sector is still in overall decline, and the big advertising bucks go on the nitrokeg variants of the main ale brands, not the cask-conditioned versions.

But don't be deceived by the obvious. Almost every brewery that's seriously involved in real ale is making good money and brewing more beer. Greene King, Adnams, Young's, Fuller's, Shepherd Neame – their shareholders are all, by and large, very happy bunnies. Greene King, in fact, is doing so well out of real ale that it now brews almost nothing else, and has closed its lager/keg beer plant altogether. Even Brakspear's was enjoying a year of record profits when it decided to close its brewery – and, contrary to what you might have heard, it didn't close its brewery because it wasn't profitable: it closed its brewery so it could turn the site (in the centre of swanky Henley-on-Thames) into a multi-million pound residential development.

Multiple retailers who concentrate on real ale are also doing well. JD Wetherspoon goes from strength to strength, of course. But there are a host of smaller chains – Sir John Fitzgerald in the north east, Tynemill Inns in the East Midlands, English Inns in Bedfordshire/Hertfordshire, Head of Steam, and a number of others – which also specialise in real ale and associated products, and which are also doing very nicely thank you. And the town centres of Britain are quickly developing fringes of independently-owned beer bars, usually in secondary locations, where you'll find six to eight hand pumps and a cold cabinet full of wickedly strong Belgian brews. Try a beer tour of Manchester's Northern Quarter if you don't believe me – or if you don't believe that decent beer doesn't appeal to younger drinkers.

A snapshot survey conducted by the Coventry branch of the Campaign for Real Ale (CAMRA) illustrates the point about specialisation nicely. The survey was conducted on a single night in October 2002 and looked at how many pubs in the city centre sold cask beer, and how many different brands of it they sold.

The branch has been conducting this survey annually for some years, and it found that the number of pubs and bars selling cask beer had fallen from 19 out of 39 in 2001 to 13 out of 36 in 2002 – from nearly half to not much more than a third. It attributes this fall to the increasing focus of city-centre venues on the younger trade, where premium bottled lagers and FABs are the preferred drinks. Nobody would be surprised by that. But the second part of the survey really was surprising.

For the choice of cask beers, despite the loss of outlets, had actually risen from 28 brands in 2001 to 34 in 2002: a 22 per cent increase, and a 40 per cent increase over 2000, when the figure was 25. Two pubs stocked six brands, and another two stocked five. And while the most widely-distributed were Draught Bass and Directors, no fewer than 10 of the 34 – nearly a third – came from microbreweries.

The Coventry survey merely confirms at grass-roots level what much larger studies reveal on a national scale: that the on-trade is becoming more and more segmented – polarised, even – and that consumers are becoming much more particular in their choice both of venue and of drinks.

Even the big tenanted pubcos have twigged to this. Bass tenants whose pubs were bought by Enterprise or Punch found at first that their range of stock options was curtailed by the loss of their guest ale right. Both they and their customers complained, and over time their new masters started offering a wider and wider range until now they have a selection of 50 or 60 real ales to choose from.

There's always pressure from CAMRA and the Society of Independent Brewers for the pubcos to offer a wider range still, of course; but you have to put these things into historical context. Fifteen years ago these pubs stocked the Bass range and nothing but the Bass range. Today, they could stock a different real ale every week.

But it's a cruel irony that this growth of choice and variety is pretty much limited to cask beer. For on the fringes of the on-trade and, significantly, in the supermarkets and on the Internet, there's an explosion going on in the choice of top-quality imported lagers and other 'exotics' available. For instance, did you know that London now has more specialist Belgian-style beer cafes than Brussels does? Well, it has. There are similar bars in Eastbourne, Bexhill, and even Leek (which is a small town in Staffordshire, in case you didn't know). When an outfit started up in Pinner, Middlesex, selling Russian-brewed beers (porters, stouts and wheat beers, as well as lagers) on the Internet, it quickly found half-a-dozen specialist Eastern European bars and restaurants in London alone – all of which signed up as grateful customers. (Visit www.beersofrussia.co.uk – you won't be disappointed.) Go to almost any CAMRA festival and you'll find that one of the busiest spots is the foreign beer bar.

Budweiser Budvar is one of the fastest-growing lager brands in Britain. Lowenbrau, once brewed (rather badly) under licence by Allied but dropped through lack of interest, is now being imported from Munich by Refresh UK, and is finding a whole new market. Small importers, like James Clay of West Yorkshire, are finding increasing interest in beers from American microbrewers (a microbrewer in the US is about the size of a well-established regional brewery in Britain). You can find cloudy German wheat beers in almost every major supermarket in Britain. And one of the tastiest pints of draught beer I have ever had was not a traditional British real ale at all, but De Koninck from Belgium, in a bar in Manchester. A packed bar.

Of course, the big brands still count. Even in Belgium, which has the most diverse and fascinating brewing industry in the world, big lager brands account for 70 per cent of the market. Thornton's will never oust Cadbury's as the big name in chocolate – it wouldn't be Thornton's if it did. Chateau-bottled claret will never outsell Le Piat d'Or. Glenfiddich will never outsell Bell's. These are luxury goods at luxury prices, and always will be. But how boring life would be without them!

In Belgium, you'll find the big-name lagers on sale in the same bars as Trappist beers and malty strong ales. In a good confectioner's, you'll find posh chocs from small independent makers on sale alongside the Galaxy and the Bounty bars. In Threshers, you'll find the grand cru Burgundies on the shelf above the mass-produced blended reds at £3.49 a punt. And in any bar in Britain, you'll find Glenfiddich on the next optic to the 1.5-litre Bell's. Only in the retailing of beer – and even then only in the on-trade – are consumers denied the sparkle (and licensees the profit) that diversity and variety can bring.

This practice of preventing the retailer on the street from gauging – and satisfying – genuine demand is a hangover from the long-gone culture of the all-encompassing and paternalistic brewery tie. It must change; and for it to change, breweries need to stop concentrating so heavily on building huge international brands and pay more attention to the niches, and the fringes, where creativity and dynamism can flourish. That's not to say they should stop promoting their best-selling brands – that would be absurd. But they need to recognise that the market needs Thornton's as well as Cadbury's, Glenfiddich as well as Bell's. It's already recognised in the real ale world. But every single customer of yours who has ever set foot inside a branch of Safeway already knows that there's more to lager than British-brewed Stella.

There's a whole world of great beer out there. So put something sexy in your cold cabinet today, and don't let beer die of boredom!

6

Whisky – Still a Winner

Dominic Roskrow

Of all sectors of the bar business, spirits has had the toughest time in the last decade. And of all sectors of spirits, whisky has struggled most.

But no area of the bar should grow dark and dusty, and any sector that is neglected is losing you potential profit. In the case of whisky it may take some hard work, but the rewards are there for those that try – even if it means recruiting 007 to help you do so.

That isn't a flippant remark; for on several fronts whisky – and particularly single malt – is making a comeback and carving out a defined and profitable niche for those willing to make an effort.

And James Bond is very much part of the move, for Britain's longest-serving and best-loved spy has been spotted drinking Talisker in both of his last two films. As any lover of the modern Hollywood blockbuster knows, nothing on a big set production is left to chance; Bond's drinking single malt whisky because the film producers think it adds something positive to his image.

With younger audiences drawn to the likes of *Harry Potter* and *Lord of the Rings*, and Bond directly under threat from the new 'Bond of the street', Vin Diesel, the image-makers have fallen back on the classic sophisticated image of 007 – aimed at the slightly older but stylish consumer, just like malt whisky.

Talisker's presence is significant because in Ian Fleming's original books Scotch whisky *is* Bond's preferred drink. Only when the film-makers modernised his image with gadgets was whisky pushed aside. And now it's back – suggesting that single malt has an important role to play in the future.

That would seem to be the case, because style bars across the country have rediscovered classic whisky cocktails, fashion-driven drinkers are turning to 'badge' whisky brands as a statement of their sophistication and knowledge, and whisky events, tasting clubs and malt clubs are all in the ascendancy as more and more people discover them.

The year 2002 saw a single malt advertised on television nationally for the first time; and after years of distillery closures and gloom and doom, plans have been announced for two new distilleries, while many others, particularly linked to Islay, reported outstanding sales.

Single malts, of course, represent a small niche market and any growth has to be put in to that context. But for the bar operator who decides to make the effort, the rewards are rich. After all, single malt whisky is that rarity in the drinks world – a product that can be enjoyed for its social benefits or savoured by the connoisseur; a drink with wide diversity of taste and a background of social and geographical history; and one that can be enjoyed for the taste sensation or can be hunted down for its rarity and collectable value.

Consumer trends

Of all spirits, whisky has struggled most to rid itself of its image as an old man's tipple, and its image isn't helped by its self-appointed 'protectors', who sneer at any attempt made to modernise it. But there are three areas where whiskies can be marketed successfully to a new generation of consumers.

1. Single malts

A malt whisky is one containing just malt whisky, and which comes from just one distillery – though it may well contain whiskies from several different casks within that distillery. They are normally Scottish, but not exclusively, and each is characterised by the region and method of production that produced them.

Once interested in malt whisky, drinkers can follow their own journey of discovery: seeking out taste characteristics such as the peaty quality of island malts, or 'finishes' such as port or sherry, where the malt is matured in old port or sherry casks and the taste influenced accordingly; through a region such as Islay, or Speyside; or even by independent distillery, where malts from different years can be discovered and compared.

Among fashion-setters, the trend towards 'badge' drinking – when your choice of drink is almost as fashionable as the label on your suit – serves the whisky market well. Drinking a weighty whisky such as Laphroaig, Ardbeg or Talisker is a statement of supreme confidence. And increasingly there are many in the higher income brackets that consider that being able to run their eye knowledgeably over a whisky shelf is as important as being able to steer a course through a wine list.

2. Trading up

Premium drinking – and therefore higher profit potential – has benefited the whisky market because there really are no limits to price. At the collector's end of the market, a rare bottle of Dalwhinnie sold for just under £27,000 at the end of 2002.

But increasingly whisky has proved the perfect alternative to style drinkers bored with Cognac and unable or unwilling to splash out for top Champagnes. Even at the lower end, profit can be increased by substituting a standard whisky for a premium brand. It is becoming quite fashionable among knowledgeable youngsters to trade up from a Jack Daniel's and Coke to a Woodford Reserve and Coke, for instance. Woodford is a bourbon whisky from the same stable as Jack, but with far more style. And it can command a far higher price.

3. Cocktails

It is a commonly-held, but not entirely accurate, view that whisky does not mix well in cocktails. In fact Whisky Sours, Manhattans and Rusty Nails have been long established. You'd go a long way to find a more refreshing summer drink than a Mint Julep, and there are several books that address the concept of whisky cocktails for the modern drinker.

Making the most of whisky

Whisky is like wine – many bar operators don't make the effort with it because it requires some dedication and, to the uninitiated, it is a baffling and somewhat frightening world where there would seem to be ample potential to make a fool of yourself.

In actual fact this needn't be the case at all, and a little bit of understanding can go a long way. There are plenty of sources of information on the subject, but even a really basic staff training session can make a huge difference.

Most of us are familiar with the leading brands, which tend to be blended whiskies – a combination of malts and whiskies distilled from other cereals.

Malt is normally drunk straight or with water, and customers tend to specify that they want a malt. Some will also ask for a particular brand. The most famous single malt is Glenfiddich, which deservedly is the biggest selling malt world-wide.

A good whisky bar should also offer a smattering of malts that cover the following bases:

Leading brands

The Glen Livet, Macallan, Aberlour and Strathmore are all from Speyside and enjoy large followings of their own; Glenmorangie in the Highlands is well rated and is the best selling malt whisky in Scotland; and Highland Park from Orkney has a bit of everything and is a great whisky to give to somebody who is still experimenting with tastes and wants to identify what they like, because it has a bit of everything.

Island malts

When it comes to malts, Islay is the undisputed fashion centre, loved by whisky lovers in the way that beer experts turn to Belgian and Czech beers. Islay's distilleries tend to produce peaty, bold and sometimes quite challenging malts. Lagavulin and Laphroaig are love it or hate it brands which attract tasting comments such as oily, seaweedy and greasy. Bowmore produces some of the finest whiskies in the world; Ardbeg is a delicious bold and peaty whisky for those wanting to make the step up to the big boys' league; and if you can get any, the now defunct Port Ellen distillery produces great whiskies and is a great brand to stock if you want to get those in the know all dewy-eyed, and for you to get all anecdotal to any inquisitive customer.

Another brand worth having is Talisker, which is from Skye and has a very bold and peppery taste, and which is whisky's equivalent of a Vindaloo. It's the brand that James Bond drinks, so there's another selling point.

Individual tastes

Only wine gets close to whisky when it comes to being able to taste the region the drink comes from. Taste is affected by the purity of the water, the richness of the earth the water passes through, the peat and smokiness that marks distillation, and the rugged landscape, particularly on the islands, where whisky lovers swear you can taste the sea salt and seaweed in the finished drink.

Special finishes

A really good port-cask finish (I recommend the Balvenie Port Wood 21-year-old, but I'm no expert) and a really good sherry finish should suffice. You might also dig out another distinctively woody finish.

Marketing

Single malt whiskies lend themselves to marketing ideas such as the following.

Whisky clubs

Print cards listing your malts range and encourage customers to purchase every whisky on it over a period of time, offering them a prize of completion. Whisky companies will give you merchandise for this if asked.

Tastings

It's easy enough to find an expert to conduct these, and companies such as Diageo, who have six malts in their Classic Malts range, will happily advise you. But increasingly the distilleries are putting together whisky dinners too, and there are many of us keen to explore new territories such as whisky and cheese, whisky and curry, and whisky and sushi. I kid you not – why not try it?

Themed nights

Put on a folk-rock band and promote it alongside a good whisky – millions of Scots and Irish can't be wrong; and ask anyone who has seen the likes of The Pogues in full flow whether whisky and music aren't the ultimate mix. And most of all, remember that whisky is a drink to be enjoyed and not a 17th-century painting to be placed in an art gallery and savoured.

Further help and information

Any major spirits company or individual distillery will be only too happy to provide further information. There are any number of books available on the subject of whisky, but as a starting point one or more of the three listed below will do the job. On a more regular basis, *Whisky Magazine* is published eight times a year and features the best whisky writers in the world, including all three recommended below, on everything from how the drink is made to why heavy-rock stars drink it.

Books

Handbook of Whisky, Dave Broom (Hamlyn)
Malt Whisky Companion, Michael Jackson (DK)
Malt Whisky, Charles MacLean (Mitchell Beazley)

7

Ready to Profit

Karen Salters

Ready-to-drinks (RTDs) continue to perform well in the trade and continue to represent an area of great profit opportunity for the switched-on bar operator. And this has remained the case in the wake of the duty increase on premium packaged spirits (PPSs) in 2002. Indeed we predicted last April that this would stimulate a shake out in the trade and it's fair to say that smaller RTD brands have struggled to weather the increased duty demands.

The key fact is that established and well-supported brands have been able to withstand the inevitable price increase. Growth did slow in the wake of the Chancellor's decision to raise duty – but the big brands such as WKD and Smirnoff Ice have continued to show expansion. Research specialists Nielsen confirm that RTDs continue to be the fastest-growing sector of the on-premise market.

Even the most 'seen it all before' licensee would have to admit that RTD products have taken the trade by storm in recent years. While the total liquor market is only showing 1 per cent growth, the RTD category is growing at 13 per cent in the on-trade (MAT, November 2002). As a result of this, more chiller space is being devoted to RTDs in top-performing outlets and this influence is filtering through the on-trade to all types of venue.

RTD is a category that has seen high levels of new product development, and it is a winning combination of high margin and high volume, guaranteeing top profits from your chillers. The challenge is to ensure that you are making the most of this dynamic category.

A guide to ready-to-drink jargon
FABs – Flavoured Alcoholic Beverages
PPLs – Premium Packaged Lagers
PPSs – Premium Packaged Spirits
FPPSs – Flavoured Premium Packaged Spirits
PPCs – Premium Packaged Ciders
Energy – products such as Red Bull

Market trends

The success of RTDs continues at the expense of beers and ciders, with the market seemingly split into two sectors: premium and value for money. At the branded value-for-money end of the market, Woody's Vodka Refreshers add further variety. These popular RTD flavours, with their 4 per cent ABV, offer the consumer a quality and highly-recognised brand at an affordable price. But choose brands carefully – consumers still expect a quality taste whatever the price.

New brands such as WKD Original Vodka Silver and Smirnoff Black Ice are expected to grow the sector as a whole, rather than stealing from existing brands. They are spearheading what is being known as the new clear category. It is, however, the premium end of the market that is driving category growth and where the biggest wins exist, so ensure that you do not lose out on the enhanced margin these brands deliver.

Look out, too, for further innovation in this category from the key manufact-urers. RTDs are widening their appeal to attract new consumers with brands such as Gordon's Edge. Archers Aqua and Reef have added variants to their brands in the female fruit-based part of the category. We predict that innovation such as this will drive category growth.

PPS brands spent £33.6 million on media backing over 2002 and we would predict this high level of support to continue. The bottom line is – expect the market to continue to perform.

Make smart moves

When you consider that the top three RTDs – Smirnoff Ice, Bacardi Breezer and WKD – account for 74 per cent of all sales through licensed outlets, you can see how important it is to stock the major brands.

If your outlet is looking to benefit from the RTD explosion, the first step would be to take on these solid core brands. In a nutshell, bar operators need to stick to the fundamental principles of going for brands where the support is significant and sustained.

Forward-thinking bars may choose to keep a couple of facings available for new products just to keep the choice exciting and stimulating. And there are plenty to choose from.

One for the lads?

It is important that you stock brands that appeal to both sexes. At the outset of the RTD market, the majority of brands were very much female-oriented in their flavour profile, pack design and advertising. Women had been struggling to find a drink that they could go into a bar and enjoy and RTDs came to their rescue by giving them more choice. Since then, brands such as WKD and Smirnoff Ice have broadened the appeal of the category through packs and advertising that appeal to males.

Beverage Brands saw a chance to broaden the appeal of RTDs to males with the launch of WKD Original Vodka Iron Brew in 1996. Men felt comfortable holding the bottle, perhaps because the colour of the Iron Brew variant is similar to that of a beer or lager. The striking pack design and bottle shape was also more likely to attract men to the product. The brand succeeded in being accepted by males without alienating the female consumer.

The important tip is to stock brands that are popular with men, women and both groups. Make sure your RTD range allows males and females an access point into the category.

Better merchandising

The first step is to: keep it cool. RTDs deliver optimum taste when fully chilled and consumers expect nothing less. Second, make the most of the vibrant colours of RTDs by merchandising brands that complement each other. This will draw attention to them in the chiller and encourage consumers to experiment. Merchandise all variants of a brand together for maximum impact. All WKD variants merchandise well together, and it's wise to apply the same rule for other leading brands.

But do move with the market. Keep up to date on the performance of flavours, as well as brands, within your outlet. Give more facings to top-performing flavours to minimise chiller out-of-stocks during busy periods.

Allocate shelf space according to performance in the sector and rate of purchase. RTDs are driving growth in the total packaged drinks market, holding three out of the top five positions in the latest statistics. It may prove more profitable to remove a slow-selling packaged product and add a RTD brand to your stock. And don't forget to make sure you stock the fastest-selling variants.

Chillers should always be well stocked, and you should ensure adequate space for fast moving lines. Gaps in the chiller look untidy and are also a lost sales opportunity. Fast-selling brands should also have space preference to avoid serving warm product due to selling out of chilled stock.

With a high level of experimentation RTDs also benefit from impulse purchases. Therefore ensure RTDs have the most visible chiller space. Statistics show that 66 per cent of purchase decisions are only made when the customer reaches the bar.

And don't forget about the back bar. This is another hot spot and can drive incremental volume and profit with the use of displays. New and promotional lines can also benefit from this.

Promoting RTDs

Again, be innovative. When you combine the consumers' demand for new or exciting products with effective point-of-sale (POS) displays the result will almost certainly be a positive influence on total sales.

Brands often carry their advertising campaigns into POS material, helping to create theatre in your outlet. Most brands in the RTD category have great ranges of innovative POS materials that go beyond the traditional drip mats and posters.

Our own research has revealed that operators welcome POS items that are innovative, so we've produced a range of high quality, stylish merchandising materials including perspex display units and edge-lit signs. There's plenty of such quality merchandising and promotion backing available from suppliers – do use it.

While it is true that price promotions can drive footfall and volume at quiet times, the RTD consumer is looking for much more than price. Speed, quality of service and product temperature are noted by this fickle group of consumers.

Discounting also reduces margin, so this is not recommended for outlets in the long-term or at the weekend. Keep your eye out in the trade press for brand promotions and activities that add value to the experience your customers have in your outlet.

However, whatever promotion you run, be sensible. While it is important to make your promotions fun, be careful not to encourage excessive drinking. More advice can be had by contacting the British Beer and Pub Association.

Ready to sell?

In summary there are a few simple things you can do to ensure that you maximise the great opportunity that is the RTD category:

- Know what works for your customers in your outlet.
- Be flexible – in this dynamic market keep up to date with which brands and flavours are cutting it.
- RTD consumers are image conscious, so make sure the presentation and serving of the product matches their expectations.

This is a fun category – make the most of support material available from suppliers to make your outlet part of the night out.

8

Selling Coffee

Martin Armitt

Some good news: as a sector, Britain's pubs and bars are doing well out of coffee, each selling an average 20,000 cups a year. This is 17 per cent of sales outside of the home (expected to top 20 per cent in the next two to three years). The pubs and bars sector is now ahead of sales in sectors like quick-service restaurants and even hotels.

More people are catching up over a cappuccino or lingering over a latte than ever before. My own company, Douwe Egberts, holds that 2001–2 was a good year for coffee consumption with a 3 per cent increase in share of servings out of the home. This is in contrast to previous years, where consumption declined. Coffee now accounts for 35 per cent of non-alcoholic drink servings consumed outside of the home, surpassing both tea and carbonates, which are the second and third most popular non-alcoholic drinks respectively.

The increase may be attributed to a number of factors, including the further expansion of high street coffee chains and concepts, and the greater availability of 'real coffee' in a wider variety of places, including many not necessarily previously recognised for the quality of their coffee.

Cash profit

The challenge for the go-ahead independent pub or bar operator now is to increase profit. I suggest that the first step here means a change in thinking. It means a change away from concentrating on the cost and percentage margin and towards cash margins.

A lot of operators are at present sourcing coffee at 5–10p a cup, on which they're making 80 to 90 per cent margins. Fine enough; but the longer you concentrate on low-priced sourcing, the further you'll travel down the low quality route. What I recommend is moving more towards roast or ground coffee or espresso (if you aren't already there). Of course, higher quality means higher purchase cost and lower percentage margin – but it will also yield a greater cash margin.

Quality counts

Every consumer sub-consciously relates quality standard to expected price. By moving from the quality associated with the 70–90p cup to the £1.20–30 cup, you'll be meeting customer expectations. And signs from the retail sector suggest that people are indeed looking to 'trade up'.

Take the supermarkets, perhaps the most 'democratic' expression of trends. Here, people who had been buying the old-fashioned instant granule products have moved on to the premium versions such as Gold Blend and Douwe Egbert's own Continental Gold. Those who have previously been taking these premium products have traded up to roast and ground products, and previous customers for these have moved on to start taking more of the espresso-type coffees at the highest price point.

The lesson is clear. Despite home consumption being an everyday affair and not a treat, people are becoming used to a better quality. And when they venture into licensed premises they will expect to be offered at least as good a quality – and perhaps even a treat.

Top tips

I therefore recommend a three-point approach to exceeding the expectations of today's more demanding consumer.

Quality

Concentrate on the quality of product. Source a quality that, while it might be a little dearer to source, will appeal more to today's more 'faddy' customer.

Water quality

Water quality is often ignored – strange when you consider water forms an average 98 per cent of any cup of coffee. Large parts of the country are hard water areas, places where a water filter or softener really is needed. We take this quality issue so seriously we supply a water filter, where it's required, free of charge

Quality delivery

Remove the problem of deteriorating quality by removing the pour-over machine. Apart from the wastage problem, pour-overs also mean that a good brew is often left for too long. After 30 minutes coffee oxidises and rapidly loses flavour and aroma. Consider joining the growing number of pubs that employ systems that brew cups individually, like our own push-button Cafitesse system. Such systems improve quality in the cup by delivering a fresh and aromatic brew, while also cutting out waste and pilfering.

Compete wider

Once you have sourced better quality product (be it roasted, ground, or espresso type) and the means to deliver it (be it push-button system or barrista), you are on a much better footing to take on the high street coffee chains at their own game. This is worthwhile, for coffee is very profitable and, after all, today's pub is becoming much more to do with catering than it is boozing. And right now, very few high street coffee names are making money, whereas you with your pub or bar have an altogether more 'rounded business', with the ability to make a much more varied and superior catering offer. And good coffee should be part of this.

Time counts

Timing is important in making the most from coffee. Statistics show that two-thirds of all coffee drunk in the UK is consumed before 1pm. Licensed premises opening at 11am have only a two-hour window for peak sales.

What's needed is to attract more shoppers, tourists and the like in the afternoons. And first, people have got to be persuaded that your business seems, quite simply, a nice place to stop for a coffee. A frontage that allows a sight into the interior helps a lot, especially if coupled with an open door and a view inside that shows a clean, bright and 'airy' pub. Second, there needs to be a strong visibility – the coffee machine needs to be in sight; customers must know coffee can be had and is on sale now. Perhaps you could use an A-board outside.

What you should certainly do is use quality point-of-sale (POS) materials, both externally and internally. This certainly helps awareness, especially if that POS is branded by a well-known supplier. Branding does work; just recently I've witnessed how a big high street store we supply has increased sales by 15 per cent as a direct result of branding by a name customers know and respect. The same works just as well for pubs. Branding reassures customers of both quality and value for money.

Look to combine branded POS materials with coffee menus, showing the choice of what you have to offer, together with any afternoon promotions. Also list any pastries, biscuits or snack service you have available to encourage further sales. A bright and airy bar doing a good afternoon coffee trade will even come to smell of the product and this will in turn attract trade – in many ways the exact inverse of the effect from last night's beer!

Size matters

Also, be aware of trends on sizing. Signs are strong that consumers are looking for a greater volume in a service. Today's average serving of 7oz is fast turning into at least 9oz. One major petrol retailer we supply is now even moving from a 12oz to a 20oz serving. There are several things you can do here to keep abreast.

First, you could simply change from cup and saucer to mugs. Not everyday mugs mind you, but stylish long mugs that can be heavy to lift and which encourage customers to 'feel the weight'. Feeling bold? Try takeaway cups, but nice quality, branded takeaway cups. Many people feel very comfortable with them and their quality has really improved over recent years. Or, if you have an espresso or barrista operation and there's disquiet over portion size, you could offer and promote Café Americano, or latte or cappuccino. Whatever you do, effect your changes so that any upsizing also means a higher cash margin, regardless of percentages.

Reading the grains

Looking to the future, the first thing to realise is that the market will not be returning to economy products. And so the onus is on pubs to improve their offer and that means moving towards roast or ground, possibly espresso.

Sizes will increase, so if you are to change your offer bear this in mind when choosing new crockery. And we'll continue to drink more milk – right now Britain is the oddball in Europe as it drinks more milk than coffee, so ensure you have milky coffees in your offer.

Don't, however, invest much in decaffeinated. Over 90 per cent of coffee sales remain for regular caffeinated coffee. It's best to keep a small supply in instant sachets rather than risk costly wastage from a product prone to slow and low turnover.

Finally, if the trade is allowed wider possible trading hours, expect a growing opportunity for coffee sales, particularly if you open earlier in the mornings so as to catch the all-important 'coffee rush hour' that peaks about 9am. And as the trade comes more to rely on food business, those pubs that make more of an effort to link coffee sales with desserts (and possibly also liqueurs and aperitifs) can also look forward to improved turnover from coffee sales.

From almost nowhere a generation ago, coffee is now a profitable and growing part of the average pub's business. The quality-focused, above-average pub really can make some money from this drink.

9

Soft Drinks Sales

Simon Speers

Soft drinks now play a much bigger part in our leisure time than ever before and many bar operators are starting to reflect this fact in the range and diversity of the drinks that they offer.

We regularly measure the quantity of alcohol that we consume by total number of units, but if you consider all the drinks that we consume, including tea, coffee, water and soft drinks, it's clear that non-alcoholic drinks play a major role in our lives. The market opportunity for soft drinks is, therefore, massive and should be taken as seriously as the beers, wines and spirits that you decide to stock.

Customer focus

Every operator will be very conscious of the total package that they offer their customers: food, music, lagers, lighting, real ales, entertainment, comfortable seating, etc. It is important to see soft drinks as an equally important category, and the range of soft drinks that you stock should reflect the leisure needs of your customers.

How many of your customers go to a gym or play sport? How many are watching their weight or driving home? How many visit with their children? How many are passionate about good food, its flavour and its integrity? Soft drinks are very important to these customers and they want to be tempted and seduced in the same way as someone experimenting with your latest guest beer or New World wines.

Main trends

In the last 10 years, soft drinks have moved on from the usual suspects: cola, lemonade and orange juice. There has been a strong drive towards quality, both in taste and also in packaging, and this is reflected in the premium price that these lines can command.

Bar managers now recognise the excellent profit opportunity that premium packaged soft drinks offer them and are making ever more space available to present their chosen range. Some not only keep a designated chiller well stocked with soft drinks, they also showcase them above the bar to seduce the customer looking for a soft option.

Soft drink flavours have become more sophisticated in recent years and this reflects the greater range of tastes that we experience through food styles from around the world. Elderflower, cranberry, ginger, grapefruit and lime drinks are fast becoming must-stocks, as well as a wide selection of flavour combinations such as tropical and citrus.

Bottle designs, too, have evolved and some premium soft drinks are now presented in beautifully shaped bottles with striking labels. Our own range of Bottle Green pressés is deliberately packaged in distinctive designs to create a visual point of difference from other brands. We recognise that people choosing soft drinks want to be individuals and that this should be reflected in the brand that they purchase, its taste and its appearance.

Adult flavours

Adults are ever more concerned with issues such as health, diet and fitness and they recognise that drinking alcohol can have a negative impact on this. Many adult drinkers are looking for soft drink options and it is essential that you satisfy their specific needs head on.

The most challenging flavours and sophisticated brands are targeted at this adult audience and some are created specifically to appeal to the adult palate. Premium prices mean premium profits, so ignore this rapidly growing sector at your peril.

Right brands, right customers

Interior design, music and draught beers can set a particular tone for an establishment and soft drinks can also play an important role in communicating your individual style. Stock soft drinks that say something about your venue through the way they look and taste. Find out more about how they are made and the ingredients the producer has selected. The best soft drink brands care a great deal about this detail and so will your customers.

Customers need to be reassured that they are making a positive choice about soft drinks and it is vital to make your selection visible and accessible. Don't bury the drinks at the back of the chiller because you think your customer would rather ask for a beer. Be proud of the soft drink brands you stock and ensure your staff are informed about their taste and style.

Consider how you can match different soft drinks to different times of the day. It's unlikely that many customers will want alcohol before lunchtime, and even then, most will be obliged to return to work or have other things to do later. Coffee and sparkling waters are popular in the mornings, while light, crisp soft drinks work extremely well with food and perfectly match customers needs at this time of day.

Presentation

Stocking brands that utilise good packaging and design will enhance the visual appeal of your bar environment, but the way that soft drinks are delivered to the customer is also key to the category's success. Cola presented in a long glass, over ice with a straw, is satisfying to the eye, but go a step further if you can. Try serving Elderflower pressé in a Champagne flute. The customer will feel extra special as you hand it across the bar and you will have added value to their purchase.

Merchandising

Make prominent displays of your most profitable soft drinks to maximise their sales potential. To keep the display simple, use a single variety and change this regularly to match different soft drink needs or occasions. Customers buy with their eyes and even drink with their eyes. At Bottle Green we've invested lots of energy into making the product visually shout out to the customer, so let it. There are other brands that do this well and your own eyes will tell you which ones to stock.

Promotions

We are all far more accepting of promotions these days and many customers will actively look out for promotions when they visit a bar environment. People are remarkably brand-loyal when it comes to pubs and bars, and promotions and incentives are an excellent way of rewarding this loyalty. They are also great for encouraging customers to try new soft drink ranges and may work well in a promotion with food purchases. Display these on chalkboards or on your menu.

Work with your suppliers to identify different ways of promoting soft drinks. Many will offer point-of-sale (POS) material such as posters, table tents and other branded merchandise. Although these can work well for soft drinks, remember that this is your bar environment with its own particular style. Don't let suppliers own your space or dominate it with one brand. Stay informed about the promotional merchandise available to you but make sure that it's you that decides how and where to use it.

Summary

In conclusion, the following are the key points to bear in mind:

- The variety of soft drinks that you stock must reinforce the special occasion of going out for a drink or meal – it's vital that your offering, its presentation and quality is far superior to what your customer has at home.
- Presentation is key – choose premium soft drink brands that have invested in taste and design. Your customer knows that if it looks better it will almost certainly taste better.
- Add value to soft drink purchases – go the extra mile when you serve soft drinks by picking the right glass, stirrer and straw, or decorate glasses on special occasions.
- Recognise the value of soft drinks – this is a vibrant and growing market that your pub should take seriously. Position your premium soft drink brands in high-visibility areas of your bar and use promotions to stimulate trial and encourage trade up with meals.

10

Selling Wine Better

Matthew Hudson

With UK wine sales burgeoning and consumers becoming more discerning, pub and bar operators should regard their wine offering as a high-profile indicator that customers will use in making judgements about the quality of the establishment.

Indeed, in a competitive market it is a feature of your service, where a little care and attention can distinguish you from your competitors, and you don't need to be a wine expert to achieve it. There is no part of the UK where you cannot access the help and advice of good wine merchants, large or small, and the overall quality of wine imports has never been better.

A necessary leap of faith is to recognise that *cheaper* does not mean *better value* with wine (see 'Pricing matters'); once you are over this hurdle you are on your way to delivering a better service to your clients and healthier profits to your business.

At the start of the 1980s, the UK was a reticent consumer of wine, but since then – while the UK is not drinking much more alcohol – the volume of wine drunk has increased threefold to over 17 litres per capita a year. Wine has become demystified. Above all, it offers you an excellent profit opportunity.

That opportunity is set to improve too, for by European standards the UK consumer is still underdeveloped (your average Italian, lucky fellow, drinks 50 litres a year). Experts reckon that wine drinking in the UK will rise faster than any other country over the next five years.

House choice

However, as consumers become more educated and confident with wine, the enterprising on-trader has increasingly upped the ante by demanding a better quality of product, particularly at the key house-wine end of the list. So the dodgy Vin de Table has been supplanted by decent Vin de Pays or better.

Similarly, the improvements in quality of pub wine have been well-documented recently. A publican of my acquaintance baulked at the prospect of losing his 10-litre boxes: 'But I can sell wine from the box at £1.60 a glass – to make the same margin on this wine I'll have to put it out at £2.20 – and my customers won't like it!'

A remarkable thing happened. Although he was right that the customers did grumble, he actually sold twice as much wine! Customers came back for a second glass of this decent wine where they never did with boxed. (See the cartoon below). Twice the till ring, twice a higher cash margin and more pleasure for the (albeit slightly poorer) customer.

DINING ROOM, APELLES CLUB

Diner: 'Thomson, do the members ask for this wine?'
Head Waiter (Sotto voce): 'Not twice Sir!'

Self-questioning

Any operator wanting to improve wine sales should, as a general rule, be asking themselves the following key questions.

Quality

Does the quality of my house wine adequately reflect the standards and aspirations of my establishment – and those of my customers? This governs the approach to a product likely to account for 60 per cent or more of one's wine sales. It involves decisions – taken hand-in-hand with one's supplier or suppliers – like whether one chooses for the long-term or whether one uses a revolving selection like a 'House Wine of the Month'. Perhaps most importantly there is the cost and selling price of the wine.

Pricing matters

Consider the following breakdown of the cost components of a wine (EU produced) costing £3.00 a bottle including VAT (£30.64 per dozen excluding VAT):

– *Duty £1.16*
– *VAT 45p*
– *Margin to supplier 60p*
– *Packing, freight etc 25p*
– *Oh, nearly forgot, the wine itself 54p*
– *Total £3.00*

Think about your own margin: if you work on 65 per cent you are going to end up selling 54p worth of this wine to your beloved customer at £8.50-ish. Then do the following calculation for a house wine costing you not £3.00 but £4.00.

– *Duty £1.16*
– *VAT 60p*
– *Margin to supplier 80p*
– *Packing, freight etc 25p*
– *Wine £1.19*
– *Total £4.00*

At 65 per cent you will charge £11.50 – not excessive these days – but 'beloved customer' will be getting a wine at least twice as expensive in the making, and likely to be twice as fruity, delicious, whatever.

More creatively yet, your beloved customer can have this second, twice-as-good wine at £9.50, making you the same cash margin as not-so-good wine number one, giving him a more pleasant experience in your establishment.

Sample time

So, get samples – if you are able – from a variety of merchants; don't get flim-flammed by discounts – look at net prices. Find six reds and six whites at your target price. If, like some publicans, you are a denizen of the Cash and Carry, grab a couple of bottles from them, too, at the same price.

Taste the wines in company – invite favoured or interested customers (who will be enormously flattered). Get someone to mask the bottles and taste them blind, without fear or favour. (A good giggle is to invite a supplier to the blind tasting – will they recognise and shower praise over their wines or someone elses?) Your panel may not think of themselves as connoisseurs but they *probably* will come up with choices good for your punters.

If you don't want to go through this palaver and you entrust your house wine choices to a merchant, make sure that you trust both the company and their representatives further than you can throw them.

Glass above

The next crucial question is: how creative is my 'wine by the glass' policy? Not everyone will buy a bottle, but wine drinkers may well want more of a selection by the glass than just the house wine. Wastage of course is a worry but a vacuum stopper for the bottle is cheap, easy to use and will keep all but the frailest wines in good condition for some days.

Time is now ripe to ditch the 125ml glass. The beauty of the 175ml and the cavernous 250ml glass are well known to those enjoying 40 per cent and 100 per cent uplifted profitability respectively.

Knowledgeable staff

How well are my staff trained up? Everyone, this author included, finds it difficult to sell wine they've never tasted. If your staff have tried, and hopefully, enjoyed a particular wine and have a little knowledge about it, they will enjoy selling it and seeing customers sharing the experience. Ask your supplier to come in and host a staff tasting – any good supplier will try to help, and while they will not shower you with endless samples, it is in their interests to support you.

The enlightened supplier may be happy to give generic wine training to your staff, which rewards them and makes them better at creating good sales. If your wine merchant produces wine lists for you, as many will, they should be able to produce a simple behind-the-bar cribsheet giving basic information on each wine for your staff to refer to.

Advertising

Are my descriptions working hard enough for me? The vigour and enthusiasm of the descriptions you use on lists and displays will send signals to customers about the care you take to give them access to good wines.

Press quotes, too, are a great aid to sales; if your list or blackboard contains a juicy Jilly Goolden quote, people tend to believe her comments rather more than those of a biased wine merchant. Also, if you are serving food, good matches with wine are a potent sales tool. See the two different examples below.

> Moldovan Viognier 1993 £14.95
> *Light and crisp with a fruity palate – medium dry.*

> Moldovan Viognier 1993 £14.95
> *By the Glass £3.50 (125ml) – £3.95 (175ml) – £5.25 (250ml)*
>
> *Fabulously delicate number from the cellars of Vlad Potemkin; acacia and honeysuckle on the nose followed by a dry yet honeyed body with notes of quince and violet – '. . .a minor miracle from Moldova, grab a bottle if you can!' (John Writer, Slurp Magazine). A must with our fricassée of chargrilled beetroot with banana coulis.*

You see what I mean? But be sure to get it right for the culture of your establishment and for your customers. A colleague years back was so bored of writing descriptions for a particular and rather everyday wine that, in artistic despair, he wrote 'evokes sensations of running, naked, through verdant woods' – which might not be everyone's cup of tea.

Display

How attractively do I display my wines, if at all? When All Bar One decided their design concept, one of its great successes was to make wine visible behind the bars, attractively binned and faced, with simple but effective blackboards displaying pricing information and short descriptions. You may have a cellar full of great wine but your range will sell quicker and better if it's visible – and clearly priced – behind or around the bar.

Selection

Should I be prepared to list wines that are retailed to the public elsewhere? Traditional thinking says no – out of fear that clients will work out the margins made by the proprietor. But people who are drinking decent wine aren't stupid. They know that when they buy a bottle of wine in a restaurant or bar they are likely to be paying three times what it cost, and they know this applies whether or not the wine is available to the public.

Therefore the question in people's minds might be whether they'd prefer to pay this mark-up on a wine that is a) good enough to get onto shelves and b) has been publicly tasted and rated by the gamut of wine journos, or, alternatively, one that is hidden away from such scrutiny in the depth of a merchant's cellar.

By corollary, if you use a creative pricing policy on wines known to your customers (see above) they will work out that you are making less margin and, in itself, this could give you a distinct advantage over competitors who aren't.

Understand that when retailers retail a wine, they are usually making around 30 per cent, or 30p in the pound (before discounts). If they try to make much more margin the wine becomes uncommercial. The wholesaler selling unretailed wine has freedom to concoct a list price, which doesn't need to be commercial but will give them the ability to discount heavily. I know of a major wholesaler whose list prices show in excess of 40 per cent, or 40p in the pound.

Help from suppliers

Is my wine merchant bursting with creative ideas to enhance my business? Are they bringing me new and interesting wines, taking an interest in my business and my customers? Are they suggesting promotions or incentive programmes?

If the answer to these questions is 'no', it could be a subtle signal that they are not the right merchant for you. If they can't be bothered to do these things, then find someone who is – perhaps a smaller, local merchant with good knowledge of your area and customer base. You may end up paying a few shillings more but the benefits of improved service will be well worth it.

Best buys

If you have addressed the key questions above you are well on your way to uprating your sales and profitability. Hot areas at the moment are: Chile – great value, high standards and really interesting wines; Argentina – crunchy reds and, again, great value; France, particularly the Languedoc – some exciting wines at inexpensive prices; Italy – at the mid-range wines, made with passion, fiercely individual and the perfect antidote to homogeneity.

Best binned – areas to be wary of

If you insist on own-label wines (ie with your establishment's name or logo branded on the label) you are likely to have to accept compromises in the quality of the wine in the bottle, because often the best wines don't have the ability to provide this service. You may be taking one step forwards for your profile and two steps back on customer satisfaction.

Also, beware of 'freebies' (fridges, bunting, ice buckets, soft loans etc). They sound great but carry a cost to the merchant giving them out. If your wine merchant is giving away these goodies, they are loading the costs somewhere else, and that can only be in the price of the wine.

Brands

There are also worries over branding. Australia, well on its way to becoming a dominant force in world winemaking, produces certain brands of wine that are now hugely successful in global sales. The same is true of other brands from the USA and France. When big business owns brands, the wineries behind them have to produce billions of gallons of wine to cope with the magnitude of sales and, inevitably, compromises need to be made.

While brands give consistency and comfort to the timid, and often big-buck support below the line, they have none of the excitement of what many think of as 'real' wines – that is, individual wine made by identifiable people, from identifiable vineyards, with passion and belief, opinion and character, with variation in style sometimes from one vintage to the next.

And if your wine merchant doesn't share the passion and excitement – there are plenty of others out there who do. Good health!

Part 3

Improving profitability on food

11

Food Marketing

Danny Blyth

Food sales are becoming increasingly important across all sectors, from rural pubs, through high street style bars, and on to late licence venues. In turn, the issue of marketing this growing part of the turnover mix is fast becoming a live issue, no matter what sort of establishment you run.

Even the most off-beat of unlicensed businesses are making a killing at times. Just recently, for *Restaurant Business* magazine, I interviewed the proprietor of a thriving children's indoor playground in Bedford, and she told of how catering was now accounting for a full 40 per cent of turnover.

It appears that, as society continues to eschew traditional meal-time occasions in favour of grazing, snacking and eating 'on the hoof', businesses everywhere are seeing new opportunities appear for selling that little something to keep hunger away. And if the business isn't going to the licensed trade, then it will be snapped up by anything from cinemas to petrol stations.

The first stage towards successful marketing (assuming all product quality and service delivery issues have been ironed out) has to be establishing the offer and giving it a solid identity. A customer has to be able to see what type of offer you are making right away – the first stage to making a sale: This is Ronnie's Bar and we do lighter-style Mediterranean food and we're big on snacks. Or: This is the Royal Oak and we've a more formal dining experience, a bit pricey but high on quality, service and ambience. This message should be strongly communicated through blackboarding, menus, signage, table setting, tableware and the like. A clear statement of what you are about sets off customer interest and expectations.

Second, there should be a distinct policy of concentrating on those dishes with the best GPs. Let them feature in the all-important centre spots of menus where customers' eyes focus first; let them hog the limelight in any press advertising and all internal marketing devices like blackboarding and tent cards.

Staff matter

The role of staff in maximising food sales is crucial. No matter how good and clear the offer, it can either be enhanced or ruined by staff performance. A well-trained and happy, smiling member of staff will work wonders in itself.

However, even the best of staff can have 'off days' and lapses in concentration, particularly when it comes to upselling in the more formal restaurant-style service situation. And one of the worst problems is forgetting to offer items, especially starters, desserts or more drinks. Even a regular prompt like a muffin to go along with a cappuccino can build a nice little earner.

One means of getting around this problem is in the design of your order form. This can easily be laid out so that the very first question (which must be recorded, even if it is a 'no') is whether a starter is required. Too often customers just aren't asked. If incomplete orders aren't processed, staff will get the message quickly enough. This technique is already well used in the larger-scale restaurant operations, where an order that leaves the starter column blank is rejected by the auto-order machine and quickly returned to waiting staff.

Common throughout the industry now are diners opting for starter and main course only. Desserts are falling behind, so at least should always be offered. Follow-up offers of coffees, liqueurs, digestifs or dessert wines help maximise sales too. Again, you can design your order form to prompt offers.

In a similar vein, it's amazing how few order forms require either the time of making the order to be recorded or how many covers are sat at the table. Blank sheets that record just mains and wine ordered tell very little. Having information about the number of customers, time of arrival, or 'hit rate' of starters and desserts will give you something to analyse. Showing you how many covers opt for starter, dessert and both can give you inspiration about what times and days to experiment with prices, offers and the like. And there is the possibility of added sales. (For further tips on this vital area of upselling and adding value see Chapter 14).

External advertising

Too often advertising, especially that taken in local newspapers, is focused on a menu listing or reproduction. Though this might be informative and comprehensive, it sure isn't interesting to the eye.

An alternative approach is to suggest your style of offer: fresh food locally sourced, Mediterranean flavours, fresh fish and seafood, modern British, game in season – an idea of what to expect in a few well-chosen words. After all, listen to anybody fresh back from a meal out and they report in more general terms that describe the total experience – the ambience of a venue, who else was there, the speed and quality of service. After all that comes what they thought of the food – just like many a restaurant review in 'upmarket' publications, which say much more about the style and décor of the eatery under review, with it's food details covered more briefly.

Special offers

Making special offers is a perfect excuse to engage in some extra marketing activity; after all you have something else to sell in the offer itself.

As for what to do, the world truly is your oyster stall. There are straightforward price reductions for certain types of people or group sizes to be made at certain times or on certain days. Special offers can be made on certain dishes. The important thing here is to make the offer in style with your business and that, whatever you decide upon, the offer is a clear proposition to the customer, one designed to increase trade or traffic among the right sort of target customer. And the customer has to get what he pays for without any confusion or resort to redress.

Of course, the more unusual or quirky the offer, the more likely it is to draw added interest and perhaps receive media coverage. Take the idea pioneered by the Belgo chain of Belgian-style beer bar/restaurants to boost early evening trade. A customer ordering a main at a quarter past six paid £6.15 for it, while a later arrival ordering the same at six-thirty paid £6.30 and so on. It worked not only for business (so much so that other establishments copied the move) but for publicity too, for it drew quite a bit of coverage in media important to Belgo's customers, like *Time Out* magazine.

You can always work up your own novel approach to special offers. And one way to increase chances of success is to make the offer apply to popular services like combos, food to share, dipping services, or else smaller dishes like dim sum or tapas – the grazing-type services that are the order of the day among many. Developing your own initiative also helps set you apart from your competitors, who too often all follow the same old lines of attack with 'two-for-one'-type special offers – surely a tired marketing idea and one that customers are coming to expect less from.

Less is more

Whatever you do, however, do be wary of the oversell. Too much marketing, in the way of a multitude of flyers left on the table, posters overhead and frequent prompting from staff, can prove too much for the customer out for a nice, quiet meal occasion. Go easy.

Similarly, do avoid carrying too much information on menus. Those long descriptions of dishes might entice and preclude questioning of waiting staff but they're also a tad pretentious. And besides, don't questions to staff bring interaction, and an opportunity to demonstrate product knowledge and depth of hospitality?

Technology and websites

Screen-based technology can also prove useful in marketing your food offer. Having a good and up-to-date website can only enhance business, especially that from further afield. Some time looking at various search engines available, those most relevant to your business, is also worthwhile.

Another useful tool is to maintain a customer database, which can enable you to make special offers direct on an individual basis, or even to issue little prompts to people ahead of their approaching birthdays or major occasions on the calendar like Mother's Day. A customer database can also provide a good *modus operandi* for Regular Diner schemes.

Some restaurants are now offering customers the chance to receive a monthly newsletter by email, again providing a fine marketing opportunity to extend a special offer or publicise tastings, parties and special events.

Use suppliers

Suppliers can help in your food marketing on several fronts, often for little or no cost. Many suppliers will furnish you with personalised dessert and other menus, badged with your logo and contact details. Then, of course, there is point-of-sale (POS) material, which is vitally important if you are stocking leading brands of goods. And through their publications and websites, many suppliers offer a wealth of ideas to boost business through enhanced publicity of what you have to offer.

Some are particularly active when it comes to big calendar occasions like Halloween, St Valentine's Night or Chinese New Year. Along with the theme kits and POS material usually comes handy factsheets on pre- and post-publicity both within and outside the premises. Chase suppliers and see what they have to offer.

Suppliers can also help by featuring your premises in their own publicity machinations. Offer yourself up for it, you never know where it might lead! (See Chapter 18 for details on this and doing your own PR.)

12

Food for All

Les Leonard

If you haven't as yet started to develop a food operation at your business think again. And if you have something on the boil already, chances are that building up towards a restaurant operation would be a wise move, for the demand for good quality pub food has never been so good.

Indeed, any bar operator not serving food nowadays will be met with derision from visiting customers in much the same way as his Victorian predecessors would have been greeted with that classic old song starting: 'There's nothing so lonesome, so morbid or so drear, as to stand in the bar of a pub with no beer. . .'

Business opportunity

For the modern-day bar operator it is almost essential to provide some kind of catering for hungry clients, as the 'good old days' of the traditional alehouse are fast disappearing and becoming as rare as the sight of a pupil at the school gates without one ear pressed to a mobile phone.

It is a business opportunity in the highly-competitive leisure industry that cannot be overlooked. Customers want food, whether it is in the form of traditional 'pub grub' snacks, a roast Sunday lunch with all the trimmings or a gourmet grill to match the top Michelin-starred eateries.

From the time when the farm worker dropped into his country local a century or so ago for a ploughman's lunch of fresh, home-made bread, cheese and pickle to stoke up his energy – along with two or three pints of mild ale – the fayre on offer has gradually become more sophisticated, with pub catering over the past couple of decades improving in leaps and bounds.

A restaurant operation?

But the next mega leap into catering comes when making the decision of whether or not to provide a set-aside restaurant for customers, and this can be a whole new ball game with an initial outlay required on everything within a separate dining room from cutlery to furnishings and then, possibly, providing improved kitchen facilities and extra staffing.

For the freehouse owner, any refurbishments will boost the value of the property and business, but tenants and lessees should check to see how they stand in relation to any work carried out, and adding it to the inventory when selling on.

First steps

So how do those new to the business, or planning to increase their catering, go about creating a restaurant, which can be highly lucrative if developed properly?

Well the first step, if any changes are planned in the lay-out of the premises to accommodate a special eating area, is to contact the local licensing justices to gain their approval. This is particularly relevant if any structural alterations are planned. Courts have been known to come down heavy on those making changes without permission, with orders made to return the licensed area to its original status.

Maybe prior to gaining the justices' 'thumbs up' to your planned venture, as with every business plan within the business from day one, initial research should be carried out on the requirements of your local market.

This should then be followed up with an in-depth investigation of how you can respond to this demand without too great an outlay, but with the promise of making a profit once the venture is well established.

As with most retail businesses, location is a prime factor. You might be sited close to an industrial estate or office block and find the staff do not have a canteen to service their needs. Their requirement will be for reasonably priced fayre that can be freshly prepared and served in fairly quick time – this speed of service will be a key consideration.

If you are in the middle of a council housing estate it is unlikely the residents will be looking for a restaurant in their midst; they are more likely to travel into town to one of the myriad of quick-service chains able to supply their needs.

Destination dining

A rural inn with no surrounding chimney pots will have to create a specially attractive menu to draw customers from a wide radius – making itself more of a 'destination venue'. Those in town centres will have to take a close look at the competition – if in the same street as an Italian ristorante or a McDonald's then pizzas or burgers may not be top favourites on the menu.

A note has to be taken of consumer trends in the market, which can change from season to season. Beef sales plummeted during the foot-and-mouth epidemic and fish became the popular dish. Organic was the buzzword at the beginning of the millennium, but now consumers do not seem so readily prepared to pay the premium for green produce.

Going green

But 'fresh and home-grown' on the menu still appeals to diners, and if produce – from vegetables and fruit to cheeses and other dairy items – can be sourced from a local farm or smallholding it gives a special flavour to meals.

One pub licensee who has done this in Herefordshire, admitting he has a passion for all produce from the county, is an ex-sous chef from Rick Stein's Padstow eatery, and so has extensive fish dish experience. He says that people who whinge about losing their 'drinking holes' in the country should realise that many village pubs are being saved from closure by incoming chefs giving the business food-led potential. But equally, chefs wake up to serving customers with what they want.

When sourcing country fayre, licensees should be able to obtain reasonable prices with the chance of a fairly high mark-up. Overall, you can look for catering GPs of anywhere between 45 and 55 per cent.

Notes on the menu about the local producer will also provide a diners' talking point. Similarly pubs in coastal regions can get fresh fish and seafood from their nearest port.

Supplier service

But of course, the vast majority of pubs and bars nationwide are situated in city or town centres, unable to take advantage of local producers. Suppliers nowadays, however, are geared up to providing either same-day or next-day delivery of a wide range of fresh goods.

Nearly everyone uses the national frozen food companies, which have gained experience over the years of the needs of the modern-day restaurateur, and can supply virtually everything required on an extensive pub dining menu, from starters and mains to delicious desserts.

But you may not want to serve similar dishes to your competitor and, again, the secret is to look around and maybe find the smaller suppliers keen to build up their business and provide you with a few bargains. A few pence per pound on the most used items soon mounts up.

Operating style

A restaurant within a pub or bar business can be developed in any way the licensee wishes, from a slightly more formal dining area, to the bar catering to a totally separate upmarket eatery to compete with top venues in the area.

Whatever route you decide to take, modern diners are well travelled and getting more discerning about the dishes put in front of them. Initially they will judge your venture from its appearance on entering – neat and tidy furniture with colourful, crisp table linen sets a warm ambience, while equally important is the staff attire. You may consider it worthwhile providing a type of uniform emblazoned with the pub emblem.

And then staff recruitment is vital, whether you are going to advertise for the professional chef and wine sommelier – who can command wickedly high wages – or try to train up your own staff. The kitchen and front-of-house teams are equally important. Diners will not be returning – and repeat business will be the key to your success – if they have been served an overcooked slice of rubbery monkfish or a warm Sancerre wine.

As for what offer to make to customers, be bold, be distinctive. Cuisines from around the world now feature in most high streets, from the standard Chinese and Indian to Tex Mex, Thai and Turkish delights, but there are still innovative cooking trends that can be featured in every sort of bar and pub operation.

Modern twists

Perhaps you can take inspiration from some of the novel approaches made over recent years. For instance, a pay-day night out for the lads used to involve several pints at the pub followed by an Oriental offering. Comedian Frank Carson's son Tony combined the two with his Taipan Taverns offering drinkers the chance for exotic meals – in the pub setting.

A French physicist, who came to this country to learn English and ended up earning extra cash by working at a Surrey pub, now has a chain of l'auberge pub/ restaurants. The key to his success was returning weekly to France to source fresh mushrooms, truffles, foie gras, duck and venison for his menu. He reversed the trend of trippers travelling across the Channel to sample French gourmet dishes.

A growing number of disillusioned top chefs, having gained their Michelins at fashionable London eateries, are now appearing in country pub kitchens running restaurant-pubs, preferring the rural lifestyle and the chance to sit down and natter with their customers about the dishes they have created.

There is the ex-chef to Prince Charles, who has linked up with Brakspears to launch an exclusive restaurant in a small village north of Henley; show jumper Nick Skelton and a pub-chain operator have recruited a chef trained at Le Gavroche for their Warwickshire local; while a former Ivy sous chef who served the likes of Posh and Becks is now providing treats for the locals at a Chiltern pub.

But this is obviously at the very top end of the market. The main pub/bar restaurant opportunities are in the middle to lower end, where the licensee (hopefully on not-too-onerous leasing agreements with his landlord) can afford to set up a restaurant backed up by the 'bread and butter' drinks side of his business.

Establish a good food offer, carefully matched to your target clientele. Make that offer distinct and unique to your business. Market it well and work hard on maintaining standards. Chances are that your 'dry' trade will be the making of your business.

13

Faster Foods

Alan Sutton

It's a bit of a crazy world we're living in these days. Do you remember when you wanted a pound of lamb chops and you went to the butcher to buy them? Now my local butcher sells television sets and leather jackets, alongside the chill cabinet displaying sausages and pies.

If you want to insure your life, you can buy a policy at the sub post office. And where's that? There's a good chance it will be in the pub if you live out in the sticks!

Giant superstores and out-of-town retail parks have killed off most of our specialist retailers. Now you can buy everything under one roof and for half the price.

If you run any sort of bar business today your competition isn't just the licensee at the other end of the street. It's the nearby pizza restaurant, the Chinese take-away, the cinema and, of course, the supermarket selling cut price booze.

So it's time for publicans, and all other bar operators, to get in on the act. No, not to set up in competition with the building society or the estate agent (about all that's left in my local high street), but to cash in on the profit opportunities being scooped up by some of the other food outlets in your area.

Take a look up and down the road to see where people are going at lunchtime. You will find them in the sandwich bars, the chicken and burger take-outs and the pizza house, where you can eat your fill for a fiver, and the rapidly increasing coffee shops.

Quick food is what people want in the middle of the day. A survey by a leading food service business shows that the average lunch break for workers in Britain is just 39 minutes, and they spend an average of £1.98. And what's their favourite lunch? A sandwich.

The not-so-humble sandwich

With 35 per cent of all value sales, sandwiches account for the largest share of the quick-service market according to Key Note Market Information Centre 2000. Between 1999 and 2000, demand for them rose by 10 per cent. And Mintel says they account for 13 per cent of the 'meals away from home' market.

'The sandwich market continues to be a growth area within the fresh prepared food market, and demand from made-to-order markets is also strong', the survey says.

So let's start there, with the sandwich – it's quick, it requires minimum skill to put together, but it can be very profitable. If you're out in the country and attract the tourists you probably need to keep the traditional Ploughman's on the menu. Or do you? If you want to have a good British cheese offer, why not try something like red and white cheddars with sweet pickle in a cottage loaf; or bring an exotic flavour and serve brie with sliced fresh fig or kiwi fruit and red oakleaf in nice crusty farmhouse bread. Sound a bit twee? Go down to Pret A Manger or M&S and see what's selling there. In particular, town pubs would do well to have a look at what these regular 'Sandwich of the Year' winners, and others in the same market, have most recently introduced.

You will find that it's not just the fillings that have moved away from the mundane; the variety of breads is staggering. There are around 200 to choose from – malted breads, milk breads, bran-enriched and mixed grain, cob, coburg, cottage, bloomer, tin, and Vienna are just a few, and a bit old hat.

But it's the speciality ethnic breads which are catching on – things like pitta, the flat bread from Greece and the Middle East with a pocket you can fill with anything you like; or naan, cooked in a tandoori oven and a good medium to fill with something like chicken tikka. Then there are the Italian breads, ciabatta and foccacia; there is Irish soda bread, rye breads and sour dough breads. . . the list goes on.

Whatever you go for, try to get away from the old ham or cheese options; if you can make them to order you are a step ahead of the local sandwich chains; and if you have the space somewhere in the bar to site a deli counter and make up the sandwiches in front of the customer you may well find it's not just the locals who are beating a path to your door.

Are sandwiches profitable? What are people paying in Pret and M&S? £2.99 plus? For a product probably made the day before and held in the fridge. You can do better. Sandwiches are just part of the current trend for eating lighter meals throughout the day.

Grazing

Grazing is the new buzzword and if you think grazing is just what cows and sheep do, you haven't been reading the food press recently. No, grazing is the casual style of eating being adopted by more and more people – a pick and mix option made up of snacks, sandwiches, finger foods and other quick and easy items that your customers can eat on the move or in between the myriad other things they are trying to fit into an increasingly busy day.

It offers another opportunity to pubs that don't already have a wide snack range on the menu or, for those who do, the chance to add a few more.

Pizza

Go back to your other high street competitors and take note of the number of pizza outlets in your town. Not surprising, when the UK market is reckoned to be worth £543 million. You could have a slice of that. There are plenty of suppliers who will provide you with bases and sauces and you can make up two or three varieties yourself.

Chances are your male customers will want the whole pizza and pay a good price for it. Women or more health conscious customers may want to share, and that leads us onto another trend that lends itself perfectly to the subject – dishes to share. Some of the bigger chains have already caught on and are putting more of these offers on their regular menus, but it's not rocket science and you don't need to employ a master chef to get in on the act.

Combos and lite-bites

Combos are proving popular. A selection of items such as coated mushrooms, potato wedges, chicken wings, ribs, tempura vegetable, pancake rolls, corn on the cob, onion rings or onion loaf, cheese bites and many others, served with appropriate dips, are quick and easy for kitchen and customer.

Research undertaken for frozen food supplier Kitchen Range Foods has produced a Category Management report into the place of combos and lite-bites in the catering market, with 30 per cent of respondents claiming they would definitely purchase these menu items, with some anticipating buying combos 30 times a year. In addition, 70 per cent believed combos are suitable for kids, providing a healthy choice that they can eat with their fingers.

Advertise

However, it is important to promote your new menu items to customers. Once again, your suppliers will probably be able to help you with this. Many provide tent cards or other point-of-sale (POS) material, posters, menu cards and other items to help you sell their products.

None of these suggestions are particularly difficult to prepare. With the shortage of skilled kitchen staff available today, looking to faster, snack-type menu products will not only be providing your customers with the type of food they are looking for, but will help you in finding the kind of staff who can be trained to prepare and serve simple items.

That doesn't mean it has to be poor quality – indeed it mustn't be. Remember, again, just who you are up against in the competition to attract customers.

Take-away

One final thought. Have you considered take-away food? Pizza sells more home delivered items than is eaten in restaurants. You may not want to go to that extreme, but how about offering your regulars the opportunity to take home a pizza at the end of the evening? And ethnic meals, curry in particular, could be a winner. Where do your customers go on Saturday night after you close? The local curry house? So why not put it on your menu to serve as a bar meal or even as a take-out, so that rather than leave you to spend their money somewhere else, they buy a curry from you and take it home?

After all, if pubs are centres of the community – maybe even the local sub post office – why shouldn't they also be part of the fast food business?

14

Selling it Better

Jackie Mitchell

Imagine the scene: four people you've never seen before come into your bar. They look happy and relaxed; they're obviously out for the evening – maybe it's a special occasion. They order drinks and you overhear one of them say: 'We'll just have a quick drink and then go to dinner.'

Now – how are you going to persuade these customers to stay for a three-course meal? How are you going to 'upsell' them, which means getting them to spend much more than they originally planned.

The most effective way is going to be either you or a member of staff telling them about the food on offer and handing them a menu. But the approach should be subtle – no heavy selling, as this could be off-putting.

You might casually mention any specials you have that will whet their appetites. Also have a range of nibbles on the bar that they can dip into while they enjoy their drink. Chances are, they will feel so comfortable and tempted by your food offering that they won't want to go elsewhere.

The result is that these four people stay and have a three-course meal with wine, tell their friends about it and return for a repeat visit. The end result is an increased GP.

Who is your target audience? This is very important and will help you develop your food offering accordingly. The pub may attract local workers and business people at lunchtime who will probably be in a rush. So your best bet is to introduce a 'fast track' lunch service where customers know they will be served quickly. This could include popular dishes like steak and kidney pie, as well as the standard baguettes and jacket potatoes. Or you could provide a buffet where people can help themselves.

Sometimes it pays to offer packages such as a two-course meal for £7.95 or a three-course meal for £9.95, including tea and coffee, as this will seem a good deal to most customers. If your pub is in a shopping district, then how about a lunchtime 'Shoppers' Special' for people who may have more time than business people. Don't be afraid to ask for customers' feedback – members of staff can ask customers to fill in a questionnaire or ask them for their opinions.

Another key selling point is to get your chef or cook (provided they can be spared from the kitchen) to come and say hello to customers. The chef shouldn't be invisible – his or her presence will add to the ambience.

Perking up quiet nights

How do you perk up a quiet Monday or Tuesday night? The answer could be a themed Indian or Oriental evening. Theme evenings present opportunities to upsell and add value throughout the year. One pub I know pulled in an additional 40 covers on a Tuesday night by holding a special Indian theme night. You need to do your research and make sure the market is there by asking existing customers whether they would be interested and also promoting the special evening. Suppliers such as Fairway Foodservice, Masterfoods and Tilda can give advice on menus and provide tips on how to hold a themed evening.

You could also target local associations and societies in the area, such as the Rotary Club, and invite them to hold lunches and events at your pub. One pub gets a regular group booking from the local day-centre and serves up food that is well received by the elderly customers.

Special dates like St Valentine's Day, Mother's Day, Bonfire Night and, of course, Christmas and New Year's Eve are occasions throughout the year that you can capitalise on and make extra cash – so make sure you have a calendar of events. Suppliers like 3663 and Brakes will be able to help with ideas and suggestions for upselling on these dates.

Extending the offer

How can you extend your food offering and make more money? One pub I know offers breakfasts on a Saturday from 10am to 3pm, with a choice of a light breakfast (cereal, croissants or toast) or a full English breakfast. This is proving popular among working people who enjoy a leisurely breakfast on a Saturday morning. You could also offer morning coffee with snacks or desserts and afternoon tea with cakes or desserts – some pubs offer traditional cream teas, which are well received by visitors and locals alike. Some bars find it profitable offering a take-away menu – customers can enjoy a drink while they wait for their order to be ready.

Desserts offer an ideal opportunity to upsell and add value. Sales of desserts are linked not only to the offering, but also in the way they are presented. If customers at other tables see mouth-watering creations being served, they'll probably be tempted to order one themselves. Staff motivation is the key to dessert sales. You could offer a bonus to the staff member who sells the most desserts during a one-week period. Or give the first staff member to sell 50 desserts in an evening a free dinner or two bottles of wine, or have a 'Pudding Seller of the Month' competition.

Staff need to be trained to approach the table when the main course has been cleared and then tell the customers what the puddings are. Make sure staff taste the desserts so they know what they're talking about. Women customers normally order puddings, so don't ask the men first. If the men say no to sweets, then the women will feel guilty. You can talk about cheese to the men and then sell in port. You need to be selling up the desserts all the time. Extend dessert sales by offering speciality coffee, such as liqueur coffees or coffee made with a flavoured syrup, and serve chocolates with the coffee.

Desserts are harder to sell than main courses as the customers aren't hungry, so that's why presentation is vitally important. Sell in desserts by having a separate menu with good quality photographs and leave it on the table as the main course is being cleared away. Customers will instinctively pick it up and be tempted by the photographs. Suppliers will provide photographs and, in some cases, like Sidoli and Scholler, the menus.

Outdoor dining is popular, but it doesn't always have to be in the summer months. With outdoor heaters, there's no reason not to have outdoor dining in the winter months as well. By doing so, you will be able to extend the number of covers, perhaps by as many as 40 and this will increase your GP. In the summer months, the barbecue season and beer garden come into their own. Barbecues can be great money-spinners and, again, present an opportunity to attract new customers. With the uncertainty of the British weather, the barbecue season can start in April and continue until September. If you're a barbecue first-timer, it may be a good idea to offer barbecues as an 'add on' rather than something special. Start off by letting the kitchen staff cook the meat and then your staff, who interact with customers, can finish off the food on the barbecue. After all, barbecues are 50 per cent show business. They are an inexpensive way of feeding a lot of people. On the downside are the vagaries of the British weather, which means they may have to be cancelled – but hopefully, not that often.

Keep abreast of current consumer trends. Read lifestyle and food magazines and see what's hot and what's not. Platter sharing is one of the latest trends and provides a chance to uptrade business. Divide one tasty platter between two, three or four customers. They are generally economical to prepare, as well as a good value perception for your customers. Examples include taco cups filled with dip or chicken fajita wraps. Suppliers like Masterfoods can help with recipe ideas and suggestions.

Top tips

Finally, here are a few suggestions to bear in mind.

- If you have quiet nights, develop a themed evening to bring in more customers.
- Extend your food business by offering breakfast, morning coffee and afternoon tea.
- Make the most of special days like St Valentine's Day and Mother's Day.
- Make sure staff are trained to sell in extras – especially desserts.
- Speed is important – ensure your staff can cope.
- Service is all important – are your staff up to scratch?
- Get that repeat business – keep in touch with regular customers with flyers, newsletters and special offers.
- Keep up to date with the latest trends.

Sources of further help and information

Caterplan Careline: Tel: 0800 783 3728; Website: www.caterplan.co.uk

Masterfoods: Tel: 0800 952 0011; Email: thechef.mfs@masterfoodservices.com

Sidoli: Tel: 01938 555 234.

Scholler: Tel: 01483 205 500.

Brakes: Tel: 0845 606 9090; Website: www.brake.co.uk

Fairway Foodservice: Tel: 01422 319 100; Website: www.fairwayfoodservice.com

3663: Tel: 0870 366 3000.

Tilda: Tel: 01708 717 777; Website: www.tilda.com

15

Mediterranean Flavours

Isabella Gambuzzi

Interest in Mediterranean food has risen dramatically over recent years, and it is now a popular choice for many consumers. It appeals to everyone, from families with young children through to real food connoisseurs.

This is mainly due to the increasing availability of good quality produce, foreign travel and, perhaps, the influx of TV chefs who have encouraged consumers to be more adventurous when cooking or eating out. If so, we have a lot to thank them for. The British public can't get enough of Mediterranean cuisine, which is great news for licensees who are presented with an excellent opportunity to increase revenue by offering their customers food that they love.

Happy times

Twenty years ago it would have been almost impossible to buy something as simple as pesto sauce or anchovies anywhere other than a specialist shop. Today these 'exotic ingredients' are readily available almost anywhere, both to the public and the catering trade. It has never been easier for chefs to source and obtain quality ingredients, so there is no reason to serve anything but the best.

And the use of carefully selected speciality ingredients can enhance everyday cuisine, enabling licensees to boost revenue while providing top quality dishes at reasonable prices. Try to find top quality produce that has been naturally ripened and harvested in season, as they will always give you far better results than forced fruit and vegetables, which are often lacking in flavour and colour.

Authenticity is key

Italian food, which is the most popular of all Mediterranean-style cuisine, must look and taste authentic if it is to attract customers and keep them coming back for more.

The consumer palate has become more educated over the years and a non-authentic dish will be spotted immediately. Customers might well eat it without complaint (they may be British after all!), but you can bet they won't be back.

Balsamic vinegar is a prime example – a wonderfully versatile condiment, and regarded as one of the world's finest cooking ingredients. Anybody who knows anything about Balsamic will tell you that the authentic product is made in Modena, using must from Trebbiano grapes and aged in wooden casks for more than 25 years, before receiving the all-important seal of approval from the Consortium of Producers of Traditional Balsamic Vinegar. Commercial Balsamic vinegar, which in theory is also made in Modena, also has to meet legislation, but it is far less stringent. I feel customers are getting a raw deal with a product that is not necessarily made from the must of Trebbiano grapes from the Modena region and that is often spiked with caramel.

It's a similar case with a classic risotto. Simple and quick to prepare, this popular dish is versatile and ideal for busy chefs wishing to offer a traditional Italian dish that will satisfy their customers. But if the wrong type of rice is used, or inferior ingredients are added, the dish is ruined. It is so easy to get it right, and yet many caterers still cut corners or skip detail in the belief that they will save money without their customers noticing.

Cut costs, not corners

It is a fact that speciality ingredients improve the flavour, colour, texture and quality of a dish, and can be very cost-effective – used correctly, a little goes a long way.

Indeed, it is entirely possible for caterers to increase profit margins without skimping on quality. For example, an authentic Italian sauce will be rich and flavoursome, but diluting it with rich pureed tomatoes, milk or cream can reduce the cost per portion significantly. Most good suppliers will provide expert advice and demonstrations on how to get the most out of the ingredients, which is always worth taking advantage of.

For instance, dried egg pasta offers the same opportunity to maximise on profit without jeopardising the end result. If made with a high percentage of egg, the pasta will remain 'al dente' for much longer, and it grows on average 20–30 per cent more than other types of pasta. A superior egg pasta can be kept warm for up to three hours without losing quality, and can be reheated to order.

Using first-rate ingredients such as these will give excellent results and encourage repeat business from customers who are happy enough to come back time and time again.

Variety counts

However, despite popular misconceptions, there is far more to Italian cuisine than just pizza and pasta. There is a huge choice of Italian ingredients around now, and plenty of recipes to use them in, both traditional and contemporary. A creative chef can be as conventional or as adventurous as his imagination and budget will allow, producing an array of dishes with a minimum of labour. From bar snacks and starters through to main courses and desserts, the possibilities are endless.

For example, the Mediterranean custom for eating little and often has become a popular concept in the UK, which is a bonus for those licensees that want to provide their customers with something more interesting and satisfying than a packet of crisps or a bowl of peanuts. Tapas-style dishes with broad appeal, such as pre-sliced bruschetta brushed with olive oil, a selection of juicy Italian olives or a plate of good quality pre-prepared antipasti make excellent bar snacks. Taking just minutes to prepare, dishes like these sustain customers while they enjoy a drink or two at the bar, and can even lead to an increase in beverage consumption, while preventing the usual side effects that too much alcohol on an empty stomach can sometimes cause. Result – increase in sales, and happy, satisfied customers.

Main chances

Main course meals can be just as simple and profitable. Pasta formed the staple diet of some areas of Italy for centuries, and it's common knowledge that it is quick and easy to prepare, popular and profitable. But it's by no means the only hassle-free option. Meat dishes are always popular, and most good suppliers offer pre-cooked meats with an ambient shelf-life of at least 12 months. These pre-prepared shanks, known as 'Stincotto', are traditionally pork, although duck, lamb and turkey versions are now coming onto the market (my own company supplies all four varieties, enhanced with fresh Italian herbs, and they're proving big winners). Served with a pre-prepared sauce and seasonal vegetables, Stincottos allow busy chefs the flexibility to add a satisfying and authentic meat dish to the menu at short notice.

Dolce vita

The variety of Italian desserts available is reflective of Britain's love of all things sweet. Popular traditional desserts such as Panna Cotta or Crema Catalana are simple to prepare and look very impressive. Many caterers for the bar situation are afraid to venture beyond the safety of apple pie or Black Forest gateau when it comes to the dessert menu, which is disappointing for the customer and a lost opportunity for the licensee to offer variety and increase profit.

However, one firm favourite that caterers can rely on is 'gelati' – the rich, soft ice cream for which Italy is renowned. There is an extensive choice of wonderful flavours available from ingredient suppliers, which your customers will just love. Supplied in powder form, the chef simply adds milk, sugar and a flavouring paste to create a unique dessert in just 5 to 10 minutes. Storage and wastage are minimal and the profit margin is a hefty 80 per cent minimum. Despite the weather, the British public adore ice cream – some things never change!

Atmosphere

Creating the right ambience for customers is as important as the food itself. Italians are renowned for their love of life as much as gastronomy, and eating is always an important occasion, where family and friends gather to share gossip and food. Simple additions to a table, such as genuine Balsamic vinegar (beware of imitations!), extra-virgin olive oil, bread sticks or garlic bread, all add to the Italian flavour of the event, for very little extra cost.

Finally, while not everyone is a natural born star when it comes to the creation of good, authentic Mediterranean dishes, help is at hand from suppliers. Do ask what advice and help they can offer you.

I make this a key part of the service I offer customers in the trade. My sales team includes fully-trained chefs, who have the skills and experience to advise on any aspect of preparing exquisite Mediterranean cuisine. And this is all in addition to product demonstrations and recipe suggestions.

If food is worth serving, it's worth serving well. Value for money, choice, presentation and ambience are all major factors to consider. But good quality ingredients are the starting point; without those you will be serving second-rate food to dissatisfied customers who, frankly, deserve more.

16

Families

Dominic Roskrow

There has rarely been a better time than now for taking a bold step forwards to attract the family market.

For while it might seem that the independent publican is at a massive disadvantage when trying to compete against the national chains and their multi-million pound family dining restaurants, this isn't the case at all.

In fact those monoliths are actually burdened by their size and inflexibility. They're predictable and unimaginative. And they're looking increasingly tired. But most important of all from a small operator's point of view, they're becoming outdated.

Indeed, it would be no exaggeration to say that the UK is at a major crossroads when it comes to providing a pub environment for the whole family. The big chain establishments might eventually choose the right direction to go in, but by then a forward-thinking independent outlet could have sprinted way ahead and carved out its own unique family venue.

The simple fact is that venues with piles of chip meals and carbonated drinks, standard beer offering and average wine, where the kids are thrown into a cage full of coloured balls and climbing equipment, just won't cut it any more. Millions have been pumped into them and the independent can't compete with them – and shouldn't want to. For increasingly parents are growing bored with the idea of getting rid of the children for as long as it takes for an older kid to sit on them or push them off the rope ladder.

There is a herd mentality about such places – and parents have had enough. The crossroads we have reached stems from the growth in awareness of Europe in general, and from the prevalence of Continental cafe venues in Britain in particular.

More than this, many pubs have opened their doors to children not because they want them, but because they need them. Families make good business sense, but it's not enough to tolerate the little ones – you've got to welcome them.

Look different

The future family pub might not be about cheap food at all. Have it, yes. Be imaginative and flexible, offer healthy options for children, and try to offer as much of the main menu in adult form as you can.

The key to your success in this area will be to not compete with the big chains but to make it very clear from the outside of your pub that families are welcome. Garden equipment is an obvious visible way of doing this. Modern brightly-coloured climbing apparatus and a larger investment than just a couple of swings is a clear indication to a parent that they can enjoy their time in your pub garden because the children are going to be happy. Any activities that turn your garden into a party venue will immediately appeal to families.

Seek out help if you can, too. If you know of a three- or four-mile walk that can start and end at your pub, then seek out local pub walk guides and get your pub included. It's amazing how popular pub walks are for families, and how many modern parents treat themselves and their offspring to a treat when they have stretched their legs!

Getting it right

There are three general rules that any potential outlet intending to market to families needs to establish right from the start:

- If the words 'little brat' come to mind when you see a three-year-old, you need to reassess your position.
- Don't try to compete with the national food restaurants. Treat them as inverted blueprints – guides as to how not to do things.
- Target the parents, of course, but target children more.

This last point is crucial if you are going to succeed in attracting sustainable family business. Children are astoundingly marketing- and brand-literate, and the big companies know it. Turn the television on to kids' TV at 5pm and you'll see advertising aimed straight at the toddler. They know exactly what they want from three, and fully understand logos at six.

Providing the ideal family venue that will work in the years ahead requires meeting the needs of both parents and their children. For while it is true that most children love ball parks up to a point, the concept of dumping your offspring somewhere so you can get on with relaxing over lunch is peculiarly British and increasingly outdated. And children eventually get fed up of the whole shebang.

The future for family dining lies in involving children in the eating-out experience, in entertaining them and in making them feel special. This doesn't need to mean great expense and it doesn't mean abandoning your pub to packs of horrific dribbling toddlers. Almost the opposite, in fact.

The European factor

An increasing number of parents have seen the way children are integrated into dining occasions across Europe. And they want the same sort of thing here.

The history of this country and of the pub within it has meant that the experience of children here is very different. Our complicated laws haven't helped. But no matter what the reason, it would be unthinkable to enter a bar or restaurant in France or Italy and be presented with a list of rules governing children.

Furthermore, it is exceedingly rare to find children running around and screaming their heads off when out with their parents in Europe, and yet that's exactly what we have traditionally encouraged from them here by throwing them into a play area.

In Europe children are welcomed into an adult environment and expected to act in a certain way as a result.

That doesn't mean anyone should expect children to be angels. They shout a lot. They cry a lot. They spill food all over the floor. Take issue with that and you're likely to provoke one of only two reactions from the parents – embarrassment, or annoyance that you've got a problem with their darling offspring. In both cases they won't come back in the short-term, and your reputation as a family outlet will be destroyed soon afterwards.

But while tolerance in this manner is essential, insisting on respect for your outlet is important too. No other guest should have to suffer someone else's children, no one should have to risk having their pint spilled because the bar has become a running track, and no parent should feel that they can let their children run riot when those children are being treated as grown ups.

Talking to children

The key to making your pub a haven for families spending quality time is making the children feel special. Encourage your staff to talk directly to the children, asking them what they want and offering them choices.

Simple tactics work. It's a good idea to have as wide a choice of soft drinks as possible, covering everything from cherryade to mango juice. And why not invest in some children's cups and let them choose what they drink from? It's a cheap tactic but highly effective – every child eating with you has from the outset been made to feel special, and because he or she has a cup like no one else, you've made them unique.

Encourage your staff to ask the name of toys children bring in, or to enquire about presents if it's a birthday. Keep a selection of treats to give out to good children, and subtly bribe them from the outset by letting them know there will be a treat at the end of the meal. It doesn't always work because children are unpredictable, but where possible strike up a rapport with the child. If daddy wants another drink, for instance, ask the child if he should be allowed to. All this costs nothing more than time, and it's the sort of thing that the big chains, with all their pressure and the need for quick turnover, fail miserably with.

Keeping them amused

You don't need to spend thousands on amusement, nor should you, because the big chains will always be able to spend more. But neither is it enough to stick them down at a table with a handful of broken crayons and a couple of pieces of paper to scribble on.

But a little bit of creativity can work wonders, particularly if you can think of something to amuse children that is unique to your pub. Its history, geographic location and the community it's situated in are all possible subject matters. But here are a few ideas that have successfully been used by pubs in this country.

Quizzes

Design a quiz about the pub that either requires answering questions while seated or which gives scope for adults to accompany children around the pub looking for clues.

Stories

If your pub has a gruesome and exciting history, get someone from the local paper or the community to write the stories up. If there's someone handy with computer graphics or illustrations, rope them in too. The more stories, and the gorier, the better – children love to hear about ghosts, smuggling, wars, killing, highwaymen and so on. You could even sell booklets for a few pence to reward the contributors, or use the proceeds for a local charity. Alternatively, provide the books free for parents to read before meals.

Involve children

It takes little effort to provide a salad bar and to encourage children to choose their own salad accompaniments. If you're more adventurous, let children come to a pizza table and assemble their own pizzas before taking them away to cook them. Not only does it engage the children but they're more likely to eat a meal they think they've prepared. Fruit salads lend themselves to the same sort of thing.

Herb gardens

Greene King's Appletons concept came up with the idea of adding herbs to children's recipes and having a herb garden where children could smell the herbs, learn a bit about them and then taste them in their cooking. It's different, it's fun and it's educational.

Challenges

If you do have a special children's room or area, challenge children to see how high they can build a Lego stack, or something similar. If there's a historic or haunted element to the pub, encourage children to enter a weekly drawing competition – they draw the picture and leave their details, and they win £20 off the next family meal, or something similar.

Entertainers

It might be a bit tacky getting someone dressed as a bear wandering through the pub, but the odd visit from a pirate or historical figure becomes an event for children, and at weekends particularly it's worth the effort. Face painting is another highly popular children's activity and you should be able to come to some arrangement with somebody over it. And if you know anyone who can make balloon shapes or do a short performance to entertain children, even better.

Summer parties

Barbecues provide ideal children's food ideas, and a jazz band in the garden with a selection of summery drinks can become a real talking point.

Toilet facilities

In this day and age fathers are as responsible for nappy duties as mothers, so try to provide an area where both parents can go to change their children. The least you should be offering is a small table with a soft mat on it, or a wall-mounted changing table. Extras such as paper towels, wipes and paper nappies (even for a small charge) will set you ahead of a great many of your competitors.

Summary

To successfully attract families can be relatively easy and cheap. You need to make an effort, accommodate families fully and not just tolerate them, set out to make them feel special and offer them something they're unlikely to get elsewhere.

Build up a database of family names, addresses and birthdays. For the price of a cheap birthday card, a stamp and a small offer – one free children's meal, for instance – you can establish yourself as a caring, family-friendly venue. And once you've done that, word of mouth will do the rest. After all, have you ever seen mums chatting as they wait for their children outside nursery, playgroup or school?

Part 4

Selling in the business

17

Selling the Business Wider

Danny Blyth

Today, all manner of businesses competing with you for the leisure pound have taken up the challenge of promoting themselves away from their own premises.

Kids rarely leave fast food joints without at least something like a balloon to remind them of where they've been and make other kids jealous. Fast food outlets go out and strike up joint deals with local cinemas. Off licences can even get their blurbs printed on the reverse side of parking tickets!

Customers are open to all this too. Most of the now-ubiquitous baseball caps we see on the streets are walking adverts for something. People arrive at supermarkets, loyalty card in hand, and depart with heavily-branded carriers.

Individual pubs, bars and clubs find funds for such promotions hard to come by, but there continues to be a range of opportunities for events and other activities enacted outside the premises that would help draw the attention of a larger and wider public to your business.

House branding

When it comes to selling the business outside of the premises, things have been a mite slow in getting off the ground, especially with simple devices like in-house branded merchandise. First moves by the licensed trade only arrived with decorative mirrors for pubs in the late 19th century – but these were fixed to the walls and so seen only by captive customers. In the first years of the 20th century, many of the large-scale grandiose gin palaces produced their own quite beautiful ceramic coasters – but these were so good they were nicked soon after being laid out on the bar! They did, at least, get out to remind people of a bar's name and address however. Not a good start.

By the 1950s, many pubs had their exteriors printed on boxes of matches and soon after came branded lighters. Although these would only last from a day or two to a couple of weeks at most, the trade was, at last, waking up to the fact that much more could be done with regard to promotion outside of the premises. The Firkin shirts of the 1980s opened a new chapter though.

There are, however, some excellent examples of branded merchandise, and the Edinburgh-based independent group of bars and late licence venues Saltire Taverns, stands out as exemplary.

First, its merchandise is of high quality. The venues, such as its remarkable Frankenstein (complete with animated monster!), are top class so they don't cheapen them by promoting them through cheap tat. Second, the prices for such are premium to match (a rugby shirt, for example, is £24.95, a baseball jacket £49.95) – again there's no cheapening of the image and an added bit of exclusivity into the bargain.

But Saltire's best tactic is to promote its concept with its merchandise. For, on top of the expected T-shirts and fleeces, and less expected golf balls, there is a range of items that remind customers of what helps make a Saltire venue special. And so the merchandise includes Test Tubes, Split Shots, Beer Mug Shots, Split Sippers and even Party Yards, and each is sold on the premises at a price that includes a complimentary shot, liqueur or beer of the customer's choice. Taken back home, they are a perfect and permanent reminder of a good night out. And they're a million times better than a branded key-ring!

Mobile reminders

One of the tricks most frequently missed by the licensed trade is vehicle branding. Many pubs, clubs and bars have a small van or other vehicle that is used for jobs like Cash and Carry visits or staff travel, but this is left as blank as when it left the showroom.

Branding this vehicle with your livery will bring your business to the attention of potential customers every time it is out and about. The message will even be working for you while you are stuck in a jam, or stationary in a car park.

One operator at a lively seaside bar I know in Torquay went out and bought himself a beach jeep for the purpose of letting tourists know of his bar and its whereabouts. At quiet times during summer days he asks staff (who jump at the chance) to don swimwear and slowly cruise back and forth along the seafront, stopping off on the sands occasionally to hand out flyers to sunbathers. Conse-quently, he never seems to have a quiet night's trading and, oh, how big chain managers looking out their windows at this sort of promotion must turn green.

Outside services

Another device to win customers is slowly but surely gaining ground in the trade: taking the business out to the customer. The most common is to run outside bars. This can be worthwhile on two fronts: the profit generated by the events themselves and the increased awareness and goodwill created by running a bar in unusual circumstances.

There are a few challenges. First you need a licence, and second you need some equipment (not least a mobile running water system and two sinks), but these can be met without great outlay.

I once had a good friend in the trade who did especially well with outside bars. At first he used them simply to get the business name better known in the wider area (he was stuck in the New Forest without a chimney pot in sight). But as profits grew (the first year put £12,000 on the bottom line), he realised he was on a winner. Together, he and I wrote a guidebook on outside bars – but he's since managed to retire before hitting 50, on the proceeds from a business based in the proverbial back of beyond.

Similarly, there are the stirrings of food pubs branching out into outside catering and independent young people venues (YPVs) running parties off-site in their name. The common message from those operators involved is that the top goal should be to maintain the same high standards that you employ back at base, which of course can be more than tricky if you are on board a canal barge or stuck in the middle of a field. However, the real pay-off comes when they have done a good job and customers picking up their flyers think to themselves: 'Wow! If this is what he can do in a field…'

A note of caution though – beware of enjoying the experience of getting outdoors too much. Another trade friend fell foul of the Harveys XB while doing an outside party and ended up – I kid you not – by being Britain's first landlord to have been convicted of having been drunk while in charge of a barbecue! He says, incidentally, that the resulting publicity was priceless!

Innovation, innovation

However, promoting your business to a wider audience needn't involve moving further than you feel comfortable from your till.

Sponsorships continue to provide an opportunity to create goodwill and get the business's name better known, as do fundraising and other community and charitable events. Best advice here from top operators is to avoid the expected. Just as customers are bored rigid by the sight of a huge tower of coins being pushed over, or a dog with a giant cheque in its mouth, so too are the news editors on local papers who have been offered the same picture *ad nauseam* over the years. And is there anybody left in Britain who still thinks a sponsored head shave is in any way interesting?

What you need to do instead is to be innovative. Sponsor an organisation that has a high potential for either newsworthiness in the media and/or gets its message across to many people – that includes your target customers. Think children, animals or, better still, flesh. If there is an annual water-craft race on your local canal, you can either be one of 40 local businesses whose staff build a craft and splash their way through the course, or you could be the one to sponsor the wet T-shirt competition at the finishing line. No prizes for guessing which course will get you noticed and talked about more.

There is no compulsion to be too risqué, but the lesson is that no matter what you do with sponsorships and fundraising, you have to be innovative in whatever you choose if you are to be noticed – and of course your choice of event must suit the image of the business you wish to project. Wet T-shirts would suit a lively YPV, but a rose-covered country pub is much better suited to sponsoring the local horticultural society.

Reciprocal deals

Finally, a tried and trusted means of promoting yourself outside comes with reciprocal deals. Licensees are picking up on this through moves like making arrangements with local cinemas to leave each other's literature on the premises. These arrangements can even be linked to purchases or admission prices. A pub local to me has such a deal going with a tourist attraction that is an indoor tropical rainforest. Visitors to the rainforest are given a money-off voucher for meals at the pub, while pub diners are offered an admission discount the other way. Outside promotion needn't involve a lot of foot soldiering.

18

Publicising the Business

Danny Blyth

Some good and favourable publicity can do wonders for the business by bringing it to the attention of a wider public.

But there remain three stumbling blocks common to the independent pub, bar or club operator: time, money and expertise. Each gets in the way of that steady flow of publicity that would have been very nice if only you had the time, funds and know-how to have made it happen. This chapter looks at the means of getting around each problem.

Time and management

This issue can be dealt with without great detail. Time and its application remain a series of quality judgements. It's up to you as a licensee whether you feel it's worthwhile to spend time on publicity as opposed to any of the endless list of other demands on your time. You decide the opportunity cost.

The case for making time is that publicity, especially that which comes free or cheap, can prove a highly-effective means of boosting business, increasing footfall and traffic and making more of the right type of customer aware of what your business has to offer.

Little spend

There is much you can do to publicise your business without breaking the bank. The trick is to look for little avenues – possibilities that rivals don't tend to bother about.

A friend in the trade in Worthing made a good fist of publicising his new night-club (adjacent to his established pub) by doing a succession of simple things. First he used word-of-mouth in the pub – free. Then he gave away a few tickets – virtually free. He then alerted the local press and Editor of the local student newspaper to the opening – virtually free. To keep the pot on the boil, various hacks were invited down to the club to be looked after during some of the big party nights – very low cost. The venue took off well.

As the club's reputation grew he then used an unusual means of publicity in the local paper – the personal column. He regularly inserted a series of messages on the lines of 'Hunky Tom, met you at so-and-so's on Friday – love to see you there again this week, Julie' and 'Dancing Queen Blonde – meet you again at so-and-so's on Saturday?' So simple; yet it worked. It brought a lot of curious young people to the club believing it to be a 'happening place' and somewhere good to meet people. (It worked so well in fact that the customers started taking out their own messages, saving the proprietor the little money it took in the first place!)

There are other means of free publicity available, such as listings magazines and 'what's on'-type guides. Call them and find out how and when they like to receive information on events. It's there for the taking. Also, local radio and regional TV often carry slots of goings-on in the area, and this too is always well worth a try.

Along with internal publicity like use of posters in and outside of your building, and flyers, and perhaps free promotional tickets, such avenues of free publicity can be readily achieved without any great time or money being spent. Anything more ambitious, however, really does require a little more expertise.

Self-spinning

The key to running your own publicity machine for the business is targeting. After all, what good might come from a centre-spread devoted to your business appearing in *Pig Farmer's Weekly*?

First, identify your target customer. Second, identify their media – printed and broadcast. This will range from the *Daily Telegraph* to a local newspaper, from *Time Out* to *GQ*, or even *Pig Farmer's Weekly*!

But narrow things down and identify the key media you'd like to have your business appear in. Restrict activity to these.

A good approach is to cultivate journalists there. Do be brave enough to call and ask what sort of stories and features they are interested in and how you can feed them with ideas. You are now starting to become your own PR person.

If it's local media you can always invite them down to your premises for an informal chat and drink, but that's always best done when at least you have a story in mind that they might just be interested in.

Meetings like this will give you a better idea of how the media works, how it works to deadlines and what sort of things make the front page. Listen carefully and pay close heed.

It then pays to spend a little time on how to write a press release. Simplicity is the key. If you send a story to a paper make it brief and to the point. Have it typed in double spacing. Ensure that the first sentence describes what's going on. Keep the message brief and ensure that it contains answers to the all-important questions of who, what, where, why and when. End it with your contact name and number for further information. Often you can email or fax the release, but ensure that it arrives a fair time before publication or broadcast time.

Building on this basic media knowledge, you can then go on and develop newsworthy events for yourself. Wacky goings-on at the bar, the visiting celebrity to the restaurant, the off-beat promotion at the club. The possibilities are truly endless, but there are two rules to helping things work to their full potential.

First, think photograph. Whatever idea you have for putting the business into print, think of what might make a good picture. Arrange a model to appear on the night if necessary, or a stunning prop like a vintage Harley Davidson bike or even a live donkey! Pictures tell a thousand words but they also draw the eye of the reader and inspire the viewer (and a good sound effect sets off a radio report). More importantly, the proposal of a good picture to be had means that both journalists and photographers are more likely to attend and cover an event.

Second, don't overdo it. If you have pulled off some good coverage for a weird and wonderful event you have dreamed up all on your own, let it lie for a while before the next one. Editors are loathe to cover the same sort of story – or same venue – too often. Direct your efforts to other media with other purposes.

And here the possibilities have never been wider. There are a number of websites and search engines with listings of events in and around the industry to tap into and see what they might be able to offer your business. Either spend a few hours surfing yourself or else get a 'nerd' to do it for you – chances are you won't have to look far for a willing party.

Both local and national newspapers often review premises in their eating-out and travel columns. Again, call up and find out the form – how can you get featured?

Or you could tap into your suppliers – everything from kitchen equipment, through Indian sauces, to premium packaged lagers (PPLs). All these suppliers pay for expensive PR consultancies and these PR professionals could do wonders for you, arranging free photography and the 'selling in' of stories to the media. Remind suppliers that you are keen to be used like this, as a 'case study', each time you give them some new business.

Another good line of attack is guidebooks. Today there are guides to pubs, bars and clubs aplenty, often concentrating on best beer, food, accommodation and the like, and these offer plenty of scope for added trade. What's needed here is a good hour spent down at the bookshop leafing through some of these publications. Again, target things. Concentrate on which guidebooks your business could get into.

Do however, find out whether inclusion in the guide is paid for or free. Comprehensive list-all guides don't tend to be so effective for business and customers are wary of guide entries where those listed have only got in because they've written out a cheque. Again, you can make direct contact, call the publisher and find out how the guide comes together, what sort of features the Editor is looking for and how nomination is made (often you can nominate yourself for secret or appointed inspection, though this is no guarantee of final inclusion). Also find out the deadlines and work to them. Remember that, because of the weight of research, guides are often a full year out of date by the time they are published – with nominations having been made up to six months prior to that previous year.

Another good idea for publicity generation is awards schemes. These are run for best pub, best food, best welcome and the like, by suppliers, local newspapers, trade press and other organisations – from those pressing for cleaner air through to plainer English. These awards are invariably well worth the time it takes to make an entry. And if you are shortlisted by, say, becoming the regional finalist, this can be big news for all of your local media. In this case let them all know as soon as the good news comes through. And if you should then go forward to collect a gong, then ensure the whole world knows. That really will call for some time in media relations and the rewards will be substantial.

So there it is. Many ideas, lots of words – and all with no mention at all of paid-for advertising!

19

Staff Matters

Richard Castleton

Recruitment and retention of staff is one of the biggest issues in the bar business. Turnover of staff typically runs at between 200 and 300 per cent per annum, which means that a typical bar position is filled by three different people over any 12-month period.

For you, the operator, high levels of turnover mean a lot of your management time being taken up with the problem. And, to look realistically at things, it means you are wasting your valuable time. Your input is better used in developing the business and working on your strategy, rather than constantly looking for new staff.

Team building

This is, however, an age-old problem in this industry, which has, over the years, attracted a fair share of bad press for poor levels of pay (which is true in certain cases). And so the challenge remains: to assemble for yourself the right team of people – a core team you can rely on.

Many operators in the trade are also too busy with doing what they do best, such as cooking or liaising with customers, but you cannot go on doing this for ever. The business will suffer and so will you. The longest stayers and the most successful operators in this industry are those who have avoided trying to do everything themselves but, instead, have gone and actually developed a good team.

You first

The first stage in the process is to have a good look at yourself as the chief of your operations. Look at your own 'training gaps' and address them. You might be a great cook, but what of your book-keeping skills? No matter how long you have been in the trade it is never too late to fill any gaps. In effect, what you'll be doing is addressing yourself.

Similarly, it is never too late to address any physical gaps in the fabric of the business. If your kitchen is continually proving to be too small, then start to consider buying in supplies that do not need so much preparation space. Apply the same principle elsewhere throughout the business. If left untouched, physical shortcomings will have an increasingly negative effect on business performance and hamper the all-important task of getting the right team behind you, efficiently working away at their jobs.

Recruit hard

Recruitment is one of the most difficult tasks you face. The trick is to be innovative – but without missing a trick closer to home. Right now, at Hall & Woodhouse, I'm looking at bringing in kitchen staff from as far afield as eastern Europe, Thailand and the Philippines! You've got to be imaginative. Try, for instance, contacts among suppliers of food and wines for an insight into recruiting from abroad.

In such a difficult labour market you've got to be imaginative. Poach if you must, though that won't make you very popular. But do network, and use contacts among friends, family, customers, locals and other local businesses. But avoid advertising, which tends to be a waste of money when compared to what networking can achieve.

Remember that, while you may want to get the best-qualified people, there are other means to this end. For instance, careful explanation and in-house training of keen but unqualified kitchen staff can prove useful, particularly when applied to dishes that, after all, need more careful assembly than complicated preparation. De-skilling can be achieved without losing quality.

Retain hard

Retention of good staff is another key task faced by every independent operator. It is the motivation and treatment of people that count most in retention – it is not always the money. Sure, you can offer a good deal with near-free accommodation and meals as part of the package, but matters like how staff are personally treated figure greatly in their choice of whether to stay or go.

It's an old adage, but the surest approach is to treat people as you'd like to be treated yourself. Be considerate when they need time for their life and, at the same time, gain their empathy for times when you might require that extra half-hour from them during busy periods. And always be consistent.

Incentives, such as staff getting a small sum for extra coffee sales with diners, can be good selling devices, but often it's the 'soft' incentives like staff parties, staff drinks after closing and your being generous with any leftovers that go further in promoting good relations – and they're less expensive.

Deputy duties

It's usually a good idea for the independent operator to 'groom' a member of staff as his own deputy. But with a lot of independents there often isn't the volume of business to employ a full-timer to stand in for you (and perhaps allow things to be run so that you get a full two days off in each week).

But it always pays to look towards grooming somebody with ambitions to one day run a place of their own. Sure, if they are serious about this then you are increasingly likely to lose that person, but then you should always have an eye towards grooming and bringing on the next person in turn.

At the very least, on those occasions when you do manage to have a holiday, you are rest-assured the business is in the best hands available and that your standards are being maintained in your absence.

Retail standards

At all times your staff are crucial when it comes to maintaining the retail standards you have set for your business. Failure to maintain high standards will mean that business suffers, especially with an ever more discriminating consumer ever more difficult to attract.

Despite how overall standards in the trade have improved, it's still the case that the first thing the average female customer does on leaving a bar is appraise the toilets – and that's the first step in appraising whether to return or not.

Again, you have to start with yourself and decide exactly what series of standards you wish to set. This means a lot of planning, a lot of fine points and a tremendous amount of attention to detail. Then comes imparting those standards to staff and setting up procedures to maintain those standards.

I believe it all comes down to rotas. With so many things to be checked and maintained so regularly it would be easy for those operating without rotas and checklists to make the sort of 'small' mistake that the customer takes for a big failing.

Every member of staff should, in addition, be alert to standards at all times. Every single one ought to 'walk the customer walk' several times every day, ensuring everything is as orderly, clean and impressive as it should be. The sum of all the little things makes one big combined difference and this message should be firmly imparted to staff. And in order to prevent routine creeping into appraisals, do vary the tasks set by staff so the whole procedure doesn't come to be seen as a bug-bear.

Selling skills

Staff can also play a good, positive role in the selling process, notably with merchandising and promotions. Staff have got to be involved with the selling process. They've got to understand it, and the first step here is having a good level of product knowledge. If a customer comes in and wonders which Badger beer to choose, staff should be able to advise, question customer needs and preferences and make a recommendation. Staff that demonstrate this ability will, in turn, be reflecting the communication you have established within your business.

Product knowledge also counts a great deal in promotions, in everything from wines to WKD. In such situations, it is up to you to ensure that they have the knowledge, so take time to explain the product and the purpose of the promotion to staff – and show them the benefits of what you are about to do.

It's also wise to involve staff in the execution of special events. I recently witnessed a good example of this at a St Patrick's night promotion where a 'confessional' was set up in the pub and confessions heard (the best winning a prize), and staff involvement here was part of the fun as much as the organisation. Similarly, if you have staff with the ability to produce special blackboarding, create bunting or use suppliers' point-of-sale material in innovative ways then let them do it! They'll drive the event, plus it will encourage them to take responsibility as well as varying their working lives.

The challenge

In today's labour market – which is very hard going – the key challenge for any operator is this task of recruiting and retaining the right staff.

For too long there's been a view that working in licensed retailing isn't a career so much as a means to the end of having some extra cash for the back pocket. That has to change. And the key to this is you, the operator. Unless you believe otherwise things will never change.

Believe it yourself. And let your staff see proof of your belief.

20

Shop Fronts: The Importance of a Good Exterior

Bob Russell

The exterior of your business is critical to your marketing plan. Though you may have a good customer base at the moment, people move and drift away for a variety of reasons, so it is essential to attract a stream of new customers, some of which, hopefully, will become regulars.

Based on a report for *The Publican* newspaper, 33 per cent of potential customers decide to stop at a particular pub based on how it looks. In our experience this is probably an underestimation. Your role in the business is a very busy one and often means you do not have time to see the pub as a stranger or potential customer might. The following are some guidelines to doing just so.

Customer decision time

With most pubs and hotels, the passing potential customer has literally a few seconds to decide whether or not to stop.

It is said that when you meet a stranger, 80 per cent of your opinion and view of that person is formed in the first six seconds. This is also the case with bars and their appearance. This decision is normally based on an emotive response: Is it safe? Is it clean? Will I feel comfortable with the other customers? Is it my sort of place?

Any sign of neglect will reflect on you and your business. If the paint is peeling or there is a general impression of neglect, it raises the question in the potential customer's mind: 'If it's like this on the outside, how clean are the kitchen or toilets?' The exterior is the public face of your business.

An attractive exterior

What makes for an attractive exterior will depend, among other things, on the building's location, style and age but, for all, the factors can be summarised as follows:

Decoration

This needs to be in keeping with the surroundings, but different enough to stand out and be noticed. Do not be afraid of bright colours in limited areas that catch the eye. Use warm colours, as these are perceived to be more friendly than cooler tones.

External lighting

The building should stand out and the car park should be well lit; this adds to the feeling of security for customers and their vehicles. It also shows that you are open. Invest in quality lighting with good colour rendition, such as low-energy metal halide. This will display your building, signs and floral displays in a more natural light and bring out the colours.

Plants and gardens

Forget the token hanging basket – be adventurous. In addition to the seasonal bedding plants, use evergreens, dwarf conifers and cordyline for year-round interest and colour.

Signage

This is the most important element of the package. This is your chance to really make your pub or bar stand out. It is often the one that people get wrong – generally due to poor advice from the supplier, who is trying to promote and market their standard product range rather than something specifically designed and manufactured for your needs. A few of the basic principles are:

■ Keep the design simple and uncluttered. There is no point having a full listing of all facilities that the passing motorists have no chance of reading.

■ Ensure that the lettering style is appropriate and legible; some styles such as 'Olde English' may look pretty but it is very difficult to read. It also seems to be the standard font for many antique shops and undertakers – perhaps not the best of connections. Informal styles tend to look cheap and temporary.

■ The background colour of the signs should be in keeping and complement surrounding colours and architecture. Avoid the over-bright or garish.

■ There needs to be consistency, with all signs on the premises having the same colours and lettering style.

■ Ensure that there is a strong contrast of tone between the lettering and background colours. Light coloured lettering on a dark background is visually perceived to be better quality than the reverse. Black and white are seen to be cold and impersonal. In our experience of supplying signage to the leisure industry, 95 per cent of the signs we are involved with in the free trade are gold leaf on a classic dark background. These are seen to be the ultimate in quality.

■ Pictorial signs are historically the most important within the trade, and the most prominent. The image should be strong with plenty of colour and tonal contrast. The sign should be unique to the business and normally relate to either the history of the building or some form of local heritage – or else a unique statement about what the business offers today.

Cost and effectiveness

Cheap decoration and signage will look cheap – even when new – and, with time, just tatty. Low initial cost will only result in recurring expense. Quality signage will result in increased trade and is an investment with longevity. From experience, to resign a freehouse will be in the order of two-thirds of the original purchase price, and trade can be increased by up to 30 per cent. Employ the services of a sign-writing company with knowledge and experience of the licensed trade, not a general sign company.

Car park to bar

On the 'customer journey' to the point of service, add points of interest, which may be decorative, floral or signs. With my wife's freehouse pub, we combined all three. For example, we inherited a Victorian garden roller, which we attached to the car park wall near to the entrance door. Above it is a sign which states: 'The old man has finally achieved his life-long ambition; he always wanted his own "roller" in the car park!' Humour relaxes new customers, and happy customers spend more time and money, and are much more likely to return.

Added touches inside

Be prepared to be different with your furnishing and decor. Bright, warm colours can cheer up a dark bar area, especially combined with carefully positioned spot lighting that draws the eye to attractive internal features. Use mirrors to increase the feeling of space, light and movement. Paintings and *trompe l'oeil* can be added to the visual experience, and can be a good talking point for new customers. All these devices can be used in all manner of establishments in styles to suit the business, from the most modern, cutting edge bar to the most homely, traditional country inn.

Being unique

A number of the large trade companies adopted the policy of themed pub, bar and restaurant chains. While this has worked for some, it means their target market is a small section of society based on, for example, age and social group; and as trends and fashion change rapidly, these minority groups can be very fickle. For you as an independent operator it is more prudent to appeal to a broader spectrum through long-term quality – you don't want to have to refurbish or rebrand your business as often as the multiples do.

Conclusion

The appearance of your business should reflect this belief in the durability of your offer. And your external signage is the one major element that can be used to achieve this objective. It should be designed to appeal specifically to the customer base you are trying to attract. It should be unique to your business, so that you stand out from the surrounding competition.

Part 5

Summary

21

Conclusions

Danny Blyth

Rumours of the demise of the independent operator within the bar business aren't just greatly exaggerated – they're pure bunkum. The truth is that, although trading conditions are far from easy, there is a wide range of means at hand for the independent to make his business profitable and popular. The business can develop a true point of difference against the big brands, and it can compete with even the most successful multiples. And this is what we've, again, tried to demonstrate through contributions from a variety of sources with this sixth edition of our publication.

Professionalism is tops

Perhaps the most important pointer of all is that made in our opening chapter by John McNamara at the British Institute of Innkeeping (BII) – namely his call for greater professionalism in the industry. In rightly describing licensed retailing as demanding the best from highly-professional and highly-committed people, he goes on to illustrate why the key to success in the industry is a commitment to high standards throughout your operation – enacted and maintained by committed staff.

Licensed retailing remains very much a 'people' industry. And this remains the case despite the arrival of so many diversions away from the traditional pub model.

Driving drinks

The more modern bar-type of operation isn't everyone's cup of tea. Often it's the sight of an imposing barrista dispensing coffees that you first see on arrival – then the eye wanders off towards a phalanx of 'designer' spirits, fancy glasses and the latest in back-bar coolers brimming with the latest alcopops. Many in the trade balk at all this and hanker for a return to the more traditional public house offer.

However, such outlets are key developments for the independent operator. First, they have shown that there can still be a place for the wet-led licensed premise – the days of drinks dominating sales rather than food haven't quite passed us by. The second piece of inspiration can be drawn from the fact that so many of the successful modern bars are independents – concepts originally dreamed up by folk then put into practice on their own, drawing on their own drive, rather than the 'retail concept' as laboriously developed by HQ operations and research teams on company drawing boards.

Finally, take heart from the fact that many an independent operator has so successfully developed his own modern bar concept that he's been able to sell it off to the big boys at a handsome profit. Remember, the big groups are always on the lookout for something they can 'roll out' nationwide as their latest big noise. Twenty years back, what was then Allied Breweries scooped up David Bruce's Firkin chain; then we saw restaurant concepts like Café Rouge being sold on and rolled out. And how many national modern bar operations can trace their roots back to the original Bar Humbug in Stratford-upon-Avon, I wonder?

Perhaps the first steps towards achieving some legendary status of your own might therefore be in developing an attractive and distinct drinks offer. You could start with the basics and get a bit more life back into your beers range as suggested by Ted Bruning in our drinks section. Develop for yourself a lively offer that combines the familiar brands and styles that people are comfortable with, alongside a choice that leads people to experiment, trade up even – but certainly have fun.

A similar approach to your wines and spirits offer would also pay good dividends, not just in terms of hard sales revenue, but also in the contribution a wide range of well-merchandised and innovative products makes towards identifying your business as a great place to visit. Along the way, this sort of stocking policy helps map you out against managed opposition whose lines are chosen for them – and are most probably due to reciprocal deals and nationwide bulk purchasing arrangements. You'd be mad as an independent not to choose to stock Stella, but offering it alongside the latest fun brand from Mexico and the newest Belgian speciality bottled brew is a luxury of opportunity that managers for the groups can only dream of.

All this is not to say that tradition and firm favourites need be thrown out of the proverbial window. Yes, we have included a positive chapter on alcopops in this edition, and yes, we insist they can prove a popular and profitable addition to the gantry. But the 'old favourites' can still prove winners if selection and presentation of brands is well made and backed up by enthusiastic and knowledge-able staff doing the selling. See Dominic Roskrow's chapter on whisky for ideas and inspiration on giving this long-established spirit a boost.

And neither does a more radical approach to drinks retailing mean that you've got to be pumping out ever-increasing volumes of booze. As Martin Armitt's chapter on coffee sales shows, the independent operator who is prepared to make the effort can reap quite handsome rewards with this increasingly popular hot drink. Similarly, Simon Speers's chapter on soft drinks shows how, by simple means like being aware of the growing demand for more 'adult' flavours and making services in attractive glassware, those customers eschewing alcohol (and, heaven forbid, there are increasing numbers of them!) can provide you with a widening profit opportunity.

Let's eat!

However, it is with food that the independent operator has perhaps the widest profit window. Customers are looking for that something to nibble on much more frequently these days. We're losing our appetite for formal meal occasions in favour of becoming a nation of grazers. The opportunity is there – for all sorts of operations – to be picking up some extra business.

And, as Alan Sutton's chapter on faster food shows, even simple services of snacks like pizzas and sandwiches can set you on the way. Indeed, this is surely a case of little acorns growing, for a morning coffee and afternoon tea trade built on attracting groups like shoppers and tourists can be the beginning of a breakfast or brunch service, as well as acting as a 'shop front' for your more formal meal services of lunch and dinner. Nobody has to rush out and go the whole hog in establishing a formal restaurant operation within the business to make much more from food – though if you fancy the move, Les Leonard's chapter on this makes clear the pitfalls as well as the possibilities.

This boom in eating out provides the independent with another chance to create a point of difference with the business. The opposition provided by chains, though not without its strengths, is something you can readily assess for yourself – you know what you are up against and you can pop out at any time to keep tabs on it.

Those who do this will make some interesting findings, and not just on how the chains seem to toil at least as much as anyone else when it comes to recruiting and keeping good quality staff. You'll notice other weaknesses too. Think about how some formerly major pub food brands were exhumed and brought back into operation a few years back when it first became clear that the boom in eating out wasn't going to prove a flash in the pan. After a period of good performance there fast followed 'roll out' of the concept, closely followed by streamlining of suppliers, rationalisation (read 'cuts') in portion size and the like. First they found they couldn't source enough good managers capable of running quality destination food outlets. Then they found they couldn't resist formalising every cost and procedure – right down to a standard three halves of cherry tomato in the salad garnish.

While there are many people devoted to eating in branded operations, not everybody likes doing so all the time, so there's always room for an enterprising independent offering something different. And the independent with a good and distinct offer, who concentrates on his most profitable dishes and sells his very own 'concept' with conviction, is likely to find success no matter what the branded opposition are up to. And, as Jackie Mitchell's chapter on upselling and adding value shows, the crafty independent has a wide range of devices at hand for making the most of potential turnover from any sort of meal occasion.

Help at hand

One major theme we've returned to several times within this publication, from food to drink and all points in between, is making the most of relationships with supplier companies.

Suppliers are making an altogether better fist of the service they provide and the back-up they offer customers such as yourself. They are coming to regard support services not just as a piece of added value to clinch deals, but as a true means of cementing longer-term customer relations. And what we've shown throughout our food and drink chapters is that there's an almighty amount of free help and advice out there to be tapped into. Websites are packed with ideas for adding value to food dishes, and the effective use of drink product point-of-sale materials. House newsletters are now just as likely to carry features on marketing your business or running effective promotions as on the usual product puffs. Suppliers are coming to realise what's more important to the trade, and we welcome this and encourage independent operators to take up what's available.

Prima facie

These are fast-moving and fast-changing times for the industry. And we've had quite a challenge ourselves with this publication in assembling a range of writers with their own very up-to-speed contributions for strategies for today's trade.

But isn't it amazing how the most basic and long-established truisms keep coming back to question us? That's why we've consistently returned to the fact that, just as much as the best possible publicity, the best recipe for success is meeting customer expectation. Similarly, even the very look of your establishment counts for a lot – and we're grateful to Bob Russell here for his chapter on your external image as presented to potential customers. In this car-obsessed society, his message that the typical driver has all of two seconds to decide whether or not to stop at your business is exemplary.

We haven't been able to cover every aspect of better practice in licensed retailing, but spending the odd hour mulling over some of our suggested strategies for improved business will, we hope, prove more than useful.

22

Useful Addresses and Phone Numbers

Academy of Food and Wine Service
Burgoyne House
Burgoyne Quay
8 Lower Teddington Road
Hampton Wick
Surrey KT1 4ER
Tel: 020 8943 1011
Fax: 020 8977 5519

Advisory, Conciliation, and
Arbitration Service (ACAS)
Brandon House
180 Borough High Street
London SE1 1LW
Tel: 020 7210 3000

AIR (for more information on the
Public Places Charter)
1–5 Poland Street
London W1F 8PR
Tel: 020 7482 0620
Fax: 020 7482 0620
Web: www.airinitiative.com
Email: enquiries@airinitiative.com

Alliance of Independent Retailers
Alliance House
Bank Chambers
5–9 St Nicolas Street
Worcester WR1 1UW
Tel: 01905 612733
Fax: 01905 21501

Association of Licensed Free Traders
Dane House
55 London Road
St Albans
Herts AL1 1LJ
Tel: 01727 841644
Fax: 01727 852208

Association of Licensed Multiple
Retailers
3rd Floor
International House
Ealing
London W5 5DB
Tel: 020 8579 2080
Fax: 020 8840 6217

Association of Valuers of Licensed
Property
c/o 18 Bloomsbury Square
London WC1A 2NS
Tel: 020 7636 8992

Brewers and Licensed Retailers
Association
42 Portman Square
London W1H 0BB
Tel: 020 7486 4831
Fax: 020 7935 3991

British Entertainments & Disco
Association
5 Waterloo Place
Stockport
Cheshire SK1 3AZ
Tel: 0161 429 0012

British Hospitality Association
Queens House
55–56 Lincoln's Inn Fields
London WC2A 3BH
Tel: 020 7404 7744
Fax: 020 7404 7799

British Institute of Innkeeping
Wessex House
80 Park Street
Camberley
Surrey GU15 3PT
Tel: 01276 684449
Fax: 01276 23045
Web: www.bii.org
Email: info@bii.org

British Meat Federation
12 Cock Lane
London EC1A 9BU
Tel: 020 7329 0776

British Safety Council
70 Chancellors Road
London W6 9RS
Tel: 020 8741 1231

Campaign for Real Ale (CAMRA)
230 Hatfield Road
St Albans
Herts AL1 4LW
Tel: 01727 867201
Fax: 01727 867670

Cask Marque
Seebed Centre
Severalls Park
Colchester
Essex CO4 4HT
Tel: 01206 752212
Fax: 01206 751198
Web: www.cask-marque.co.uk
Email: cask-marque@mcno.com

Catering Equipment Distributors
Association (CEDA)
PO Box 194
Bingley
West Yorks BD16 2XW
Tel: 01274 826056
Fax: 01274 777260
Email: secretary@ceda.co.uk

Catering Equipment Supplies
Association (CESA)
Carlyle House
235–237 Vauxhall Bridge Road
London SW1V 1EL
Tel: 020 7233 7724
Fax: 020 7828 0667
Web: www.cesa.org.uk

Chartered Institute of Environmental
Health
Chadwick Court
15 Hatfields
London SE1 8DJ
Tel: 020 7928 6006
Fax: 020 7827 5865

City and Guilds
1 Giltspur Street
London EC1A 9DD
Tel: 020 7294 2468
Fax: 020 7294 2400

Cleaning & Hygiene Suppliers
Association
PO Box 770
Marlow
Bucks SL7 2SH
Tel: 01628 478273

Confederation of Tourism, Hotel and
Catering Management
118–120 Great Titchfield Street
London W1P 7AJ
Tel/Fax: 020 7612 0170

Cookery and Food Association
1 Victoria Parade
331 Sandycombe Road
Richmond
Surrey TW9 3NB
Tel: 020 8948 3870
Fax: 020 8332 6326

Department for Work and Pensions
Richmond House
79 Whitehall
London SW1A 2NS
Tel: 020 7210 3000

Employment Rights Advice Service
27–29 Amwell Street
London EC1R 1TL
Tel: 020 7713 7583

English Tourism Council
Thames Tower
Blacks Road
London W6 9EL
Tel: 020 8563 3000
Fax: 020 8563 0302

English Wine Society
Vine House
Glade Road
Marlow
Bucks SL7 1DZ
Tel: 01628 482299

Federation of Licensed Victuallers'
Associations
126 Bradford Road
Brighouse
West Yorks HD6 4AU
Tel: 01484 710534
Fax: 01484 718647

Federation of Retail Licensed Trade
91 University Street
Belfast BT7 1HP
Tel/Fax: 028 9032 7578

Food From Britain
123 Buckingham Palace Road
London SW1W 9SA
Tel: 020 7233 5111

Guild of Master Victuallers
Royal Six Bells
222 High Street
Colliers Wood
London SW19 2BH
Tel: 020 7222 5300

Health and Safety Executive
Information Services
Broad Lane
Sheffield
South Yorks S3 7HQ
Tel: 0541 545500
Fax: 0114 289 2333

HM Customs & Excise
Dorset House
Stamford Street
London SE1 9PY
Tel: 020 7928 3344

Hospitality Training Foundation
International House
3rd Floor
High Street
Ealing
London W5 5DB
Tel: 020 8579 2400
Fax: 020 8840 6217

HSE Books
PO Box 1999
Sudbury
Suffolk CO10 2WA
Tel: 01787 881165

Licensed Retail Consultants
(Paul Cooper)
46 Front Street
Slip End
Luton
Bedfordshire
Tel: 01582 424484

Licensed Trade Charities Trust
The Brows, Sutton Place
Abinger Hammer
Dorking
Surrey RH5 6RL
Tel: 01306 731223

Licensed Victuallers' Trade
Association (London & south east)
Royal Six Bells
222 High Street
Colliers Wood
London SW19 2BH
Tel: 020 8540 1275
Fax: 020 8540 2715

Licensed Victuallers' Trade
Association (Midlands)
Larkfield
Ashlawn Road
Rugby CV22 5QE
Tel: 01788 553353
Fax: 01788 535626

Licensed Victuallers' Trade
Association (West)
The Benett Arms
Semley Nr Shaftesbury
Dorset SP7 9AS
Tel: 01747 830221
Fax: 01747 830152

Licensed Victuallers Wales
2 Derwendeg Station Road
Govilon
Abergavenny
Gwent NP7 9RG
Tel/Fax: 01873 830415

London Tourist Board
Glen House, Stag Place
London SW1E 5LT
Tel: 020 7932 2000

Music Alliance
29–33 Berners Street
London W1P 4AA
Tel: 020 7580 5544
Fax: 020 7306 4050

National Pubwatch
17 Chace Avenue
Potters Bar
Hertfordshire
EN6 5LX
Tel: 01707 650095
Email: m.eidmans@btinternet.com

Office of Fair Trading
Field House
15–25 Breams Buildings
London EC4A 1PR
Tel: 020 7211 8000

Pannone & Partners
123 Deansgate
Manchester M3 2BU
Tel: 0161 909 3000
Fax: 0161 909 4444

Performing Rights Society
29–33 Berners Street
London W1P 4AA
Tel: 020 7580 5544

Portman Group
7–10 Chandos Street
London W1G 9DQ
Tel: 020 7907 3700
Fax: 020 7907 3710
Web: www.portman-group.org.uk
Email: info@portman-group.org.uk

Restaurant Association
Africa House
64–78 Kingsway
London WC2B 6AH
Tel: 020 7831 8727

Royal Society for the Prevention of
Accidents (RoSPA)
Edgbaston Park
353 Bristol Road
Birmingham B5 7ST
Tel: 0121 248 2000
Fax: 0121 248 2001

Scottish Licensed Trade Association
10 Walker Street
Edinburgh EH3 7LA
Tel: 0131 225 5169
Fax: 0131 220 4057

Scottish Tourist Board
23 Ravelston Terrace
Edinburgh EH4 3TP
Tel: 0131 332 2433
Fax: 0131 343 1513

Society of Licensed Victuallers
Heatherley
London Road
Ascot SL5 8DR
Tel: 01344 844440

Sussex Society of Licensed Victuallers
Pearn House, 98 Riley Road
Brighton
East Sussex BN2 2AH
Tel: 01273 682743

The Tourism Society
26 Chapter Street
London SW1P 4ND
Tel: 020 7834 0461

The Vegetarian Society
Parkdale, Dunham Road
Altrincham
Cheshire
WA14 4QG
Tel: 0161 925 2000

Wales Tourist Board
Brunel House
2 Fitzalan Road
Cardiff CF24 0UY
Tel: 029 2049 9909
Fax: 029 2048 5031

Wine & Spirit Education Trust
Five Kings House
1 Queen Street Place
London EC4R 1QS
Tel: 020 7236 3551
Fax: 020 7329 8712

Index of advertisers